1/94

MENTAL RETARDATION

GENERAL EDITORS

Dale C. Garell, M.D.
Medical Director, California Children Services, Department of Health Services,
  County of Los Angeles
Associate Dean for Curriculum; Clinical Professor, Department of Pediatrics &
  Family Medicine, University of Southern California School of Medicine
Former President, Society for Adolescent Medicine

Solomon H. Snyder, M.D.
Distinguished Service Professor of Neuroscience, Pharmacology, and Psychiatry,
  Johns Hopkins University School of Medicine
Former President, Society for Neuroscience
Albert Lasker Award in Medical Research, 1978

CONSULTING EDITORS

Robert W. Blum, M.D., Ph.D.
Professor and Director, Division of General Pediatrics and Adolescent Health,
  University of Minnesota

Charles E. Irwin, Jr., M.D.
Professor of Pediatrics; Director, Division of Adolescent Medicine, University of
  California, San Francisco

Lloyd J. Kolbe, Ph.D.
Director of the Division of Adolescent and School Health, Center for Chronic
  Disease Prevention and Health Promotion, Centers for Disease Control

Jordan J. Popkin
Former Director, Division of Federal Employee Occupational Health, U.S. Public
  Health Service Region I

Joseph L. Rauh, M.D.
Professor of Pediatrics and Medicine, Adolescent Medicine, Children's Hospital
  Medical Center, Cincinnati
Former President, Society for Adolescent Medicine

THE ENCYCLOPEDIA OF
H E A L T H

PSYCHOLOGICAL DISORDERS
AND THEIR TREATMENT

Dale C. Garell, M.D. · General Editor

MENTAL RETARDATION

LAURA DOLCE

Introduction by C. Everett Koop, M.D., Sc.D.

former Surgeon General, U. S. Public Health Service

CHELSEA HOUSE PUBLISHERS

New York · Philadelphia

The goal of the ENCYCLOPEDIA OF HEALTH *is to provide general information in the ever-changing areas of physiology, psychology, and related medical issues. The titles in this series are not intended to take the place of the professional advice of a physician or other health care professional.*

CHELSEA HOUSE PUBLISHERS
EDITORIAL DIRECTOR   Richard Rennert
EXECUTIVE MANAGING EDITOR   Karyn Gullen Browne
EXECUTIVE EDITOR   Sean Dolan
COPY CHIEF   Robin James
PICTURE EDITOR   Adrian G. Allen
MANUFACTURING DIRECTOR   Gerald Levine
SYSTEMS MANAGER   Lindsey Ottman
PRODUCTION COORDINATOR   Marie Claire Cebrián-Ume

The Encyclopedia of Health
SENIOR EDITOR   Kenneth W. Lane

Staff for MENTAL RETARDATION
COPY EDITOR   David Carter
EDITORIAL ASSISTANT   Mary B. Sisson
PICTURE RESEARCHER   Sandy Jones
DESIGNER   M. Cambraia Magalhães

First Printing
1   3   5   7   9   8   6   4   2

Library of Congress Cataloging-in-Publication Data

Dolce, Laura
  Mental Retardation/by Laura Dolce; introduction by C. Everett Koop.
    p. cm.— (The Encyclopedia of health)
  Includes bibliographical references and index.
  Summary: An examination of mental retardation, including its history, how it occurs, and methods of education and treatment.
  ISBN 0-7910-0050-8
        0-7910-0530-5 (pbk.)
  1. Mental retardation—Juvenile literature. [1. Mentally handicapped. 2. Learning disabilities.] I. Title. II. Series.
RC570.D63 1993   92-32087
616.85'88 — dc20   CIP
                                                                               AC

CONTENTS

THE ENCYCLOPEDIA OF
H E A L T H

THE HEALTHY BODY

The Circulatory System
Dental Health
The Digestive System
The Endocrine System
Exercise
Genetics & Heredity
The Human Body: An Overview
Hygiene
The Immune System
Memory & Learning
The Musculoskeletal System
The Nervous System
Nutrition
The Reproductive System
The Respiratory System
The Senses
Sleep
Speech & Hearing
Sports Medicine
Vision
Vitamins & Minerals

THE LIFE CYCLE

Adolescence
Adulthood
Aging
Childhood
Death & Dying
The Family
Friendship & Love
Pregnancy & Birth

MEDICAL ISSUES

Careers in Health Care
Environmental Health
Folk Medicine
Health Care Delivery
Holistic Medicine
Medical Ethics
Medical Fakes & Frauds
Medical Technology
Medicine & the Law
Occupational Health
Public Health

PSYCHOLOGICAL DISORDERS AND THEIR TREATMENT

Anxiety & Phobias
Child Abuse
Compulsive Behavior
Delinquency & Criminal Behavior
Depression
Diagnosing & Treating Mental Illness
Eating Habits & Disorders
Learning Disabilities
Mental Retardation
Personality Disorders
Schizophrenia
Stress Management
Suicide

MEDICAL DISORDERS AND THEIR TREATMENT

AIDS
Allergies
Alzheimer's Disease
Arthritis
Birth Defects
Cancer
The Common Cold
Diabetes
Emergency Medicine
Gynecological Disorders
Headaches
The Hospital
Kidney Disorders
Medical Diagnosis
The Mind-Body Connection
Mononucleosis and Other Infectious Diseases
Nuclear Medicine
Organ Transplants
Pain
Physical Handicaps
Poisons & Toxins
Prescription & OTC Drugs
Sexually Transmitted Diseases
Skin Disorders
Stroke & Heart Disease
Substance Abuse
Tropical Medicine

PREVENTION AND EDUCATION: THE KEYS TO GOOD HEALTH

C. Everett Koop, M.D., Sc.D.
former Surgeon General,
U.S. Public Health Service

The issue of health education has received particular attention in recent years because of the presence of AIDS in the news. But our response to this particular tragedy points up a number of broader issues that doctors, public health officials, educators, and the public face. In particular, it points up the necessity for sound health education for citizens of all ages.

Over the past 25 years this country has been able to bring about dramatic declines in the death rates for heart disease, stroke, accidents, and for people under the age of 45, cancer. Today, Americans generally eat better and take better care of themselves than ever before. Thus, with the help of modern science and technology, they have a better chance of surviving serious—even catastrophic—illnesses. That's the good news.

But, like every phonograph record, there's a flip side, and one with special significance for young adults. According to a report issued in 1979 by Dr. Julius Richmond, my predecessor as Surgeon General, Americans aged 15 to 24 had a higher death rate in 1979 than they did 20 years earlier. The causes: violent death and injury, alcohol and drug abuse, unwanted pregnancies, and sexually transmitted diseases. Adolescents are particularly vulnerable because they are beginning to explore their own sexuality and perhaps to experiment with drugs. The need for educating young people is critical, and the price of neglect is high.

Yet even for the population as a whole, our health is still far from what it could be. Why? A 1974 Canadian government report attributed all death and disease to four broad elements: inadequacies in the health care system, behavioral factors or unhealthy life-styles, environmental hazards, and human biological factors.

To be sure, there are diseases that are still beyond the control of even our advanced medical knowledge and techniques. And despite yearnings that are as old as the human race itself, there is no "fountain of youth" to ward off aging and death. Still, there is a solution to many of the problems that undermine sound health. In a word, that solution is prevention. Prevention, which includes health promotion and education, saves lives, improves the quality of life, and in the long run, saves money.

In the United States, organized public health activities and preventive medicine have a long history. Important milestones in this country or foreign breakthroughs adopted in the United States include the improvement of sanitary procedures and the development of pasteurized milk in the late 19th century and the introduction in the mid-20th century of effective vaccines against polio, measles, German measles, mumps, and other once-rampant diseases. Internationally, organized public health efforts began on a wide-scale basis with the International Sanitary Conference of 1851, to which 12 nations sent representatives. The World Health Organization, founded in 1948, continues these efforts under the aegis of the United Nations, with particular emphasis on combating communicable diseases and the training of health care workers.

Despite these accomplishments, much remains to be done in the field of prevention. For too long, we have had a medical care system that is science- and technology-based, focused, essentially, on illness and mortality. It is now patently obvious that both the social and the economic costs of such a system are becoming insupportable.

Implementing prevention—and its corollaries, health education and promotion—is the job of several groups of people.

First, the medical and scientific professions need to continue basic scientific research, and here we are making considerable progress. But increased concern with prevention will also have a decided impact on how primary care doctors practice medicine. With a shift to health-based rather than morbidity-based medicine, the role of the "new physician" will include a healthy dose of patient education.

Second, practitioners of the social and behavioral sciences—psychologists, economists, city planners—along with lawyers, business leaders, and government officials—must solve the practical and ethical dilemmas confronting us: poverty, crime, civil rights, literacy, education, employment, housing, sanitation, environmental protection, health care delivery systems, and so forth. All of these issues affect public health.

Third is the public at large. We'll consider that very important group in a moment.

Fourth, and the linchpin in this effort, is the public health profession—doctors, epidemiologists, teachers—who must harness the professional expertise of the first two groups and the common sense and cooperation of the third, the public. They must define the problems statistically and qualitatively and then help us set priorities for finding the solutions.

To a very large extent, improving those statistics is the responsibility of every individual. So let's consider more specifically what the role of the individual should be and why health education is so important to that role. First, and most obvious, individuals can protect themselves from illness and injury and thus minimize their need for professional medical care. They can eat nutritious food; get adequate exercise; avoid tobacco, alcohol, and drugs; and take prudent steps to avoid accidents. The proverbial "apple a day keeps the doctor away" is not so far from the truth, after all.

Second, individuals should actively participate in their own medical care. They should schedule regular medical and dental checkups. Should they develop an illness or injury, they should know when to treat themselves and when to seek professional help. To gain the maximum benefit from any medical treatment that they do require, individuals must become partners in that treatment. For instance, they should understand the effects and side effects of medications. I counsel young physicians that there is no such thing as too much information when talking with patients. But the corollary is the patient must know enough about the nuts and bolts of the healing process to understand what the doctor is telling him or her. That is at least partially the patient's responsibility.

Education is equally necessary for us to understand the ethical and public policy issues in health care today. Sometimes individuals will encounter these issues in making decisions about their own treatment or that of family members. Other citizens may encounter them as jurors in medical malpractice cases. But we all become involved, indirectly, when we elect our public officials, from school board members to the president. Should surrogate parenting be legal? To what extent is drug testing desirable, legal, or necessary? Should there be public funding for family planning, hospitals, various types of medical research, and other medical care for the indigent? How should we allocate scant technological resources, such as kidney dialysis and organ transplants? What is the proper role of government in protecting the rights of patients?

What are the broad goals of public health in the United States today? In 1980, the Public Health Service issued a report aptly entitled *Promoting Health—Preventing Disease: Objectives for the Nation*. This report expressed its goals in terms of mortality and in terms of intermediate goals in education and health improvement. It identified 15 major concerns: controlling high blood pressure; improving family planning; improving pregnancy care and infant health; increasing the rate of immunization; controlling sexually transmitted diseases; controlling the presence of toxic agents and radiation in the environment; improving occupational safety and health; preventing accidents; promoting water fluoridation and dental health; controlling infectious diseases; decreasing smoking; decreasing alcohol and drug abuse; improving nutrition; promoting physical fitness and exercise; and controlling stress and violent behavior.

For healthy adolescents and young adults (ages 15 to 24), the specific goal was a 20% reduction in deaths, with a special focus on motor vehicle injuries and alcohol and drug abuse. For adults (ages 25 to 64), the aim was 25% fewer deaths, with a concentration on heart attacks, strokes, and cancers.

Smoking is perhaps the best example of how individual behavior can have a direct impact on health. Today, cigarette smoking is recognized as the single most important preventable cause of death in our society. It is responsible for more cancers and more cancer deaths than any other known agent; is a prime risk factor for heart and blood vessel disease, chronic bronchitis, and emphysema; and is a frequent cause of complications in pregnancies and of babies born prematurely, underweight, or with potentially fatal respiratory and cardiovascular problems.

Since the release of the Surgeon General's first report on smoking in 1964, the proportion of adult smokers has declined substantially, from 43% in 1965 to 30.5% in 1985. Since 1965, 37 million people have quit smoking. Although there is still much work to be done if we are to become a "smoke-free society," it is heartening to note that public health and public education efforts—such as warnings on cigarette packages and bans on broadcast advertising—have already had significant effects.

In 1835, Alexis de Tocqueville, a French visitor to America, wrote, "In America the passion for physical well-being is general." Today, as then, health and fitness are front-page items. But with the greater scientific and technological resources now available to us, we are in a far stronger position to make good health care available to everyone. And with the greater technological threats to us as we approach the 21st century, the need to do so is more urgent than ever before. Comprehensive information about basic biology, preventive medicine, medical and surgical treatments, and related ethical and public policy issues can help you arm yourself with the knowledge you need to be healthy throughout your life.

FOREWORD

Dale C. Garell, M.D.

A dvances in our understanding of health and disease during the 20th century have been truly remarkable. Indeed, it could be argued that modern health care is one of the greatest accomplishments in all of human history. In the early 20th century, improvements in sanitation, water treatment, and sewage disposal reduced death rates and increased longevity. Previously untreatable illnesses can now be managed with antibiotics, immunizations, and modern surgical techniques. Discoveries in the fields of immunology, genetic diagnosis, and organ transplantation are revolutionizing the prevention and treatment of disease. Modern medicine is even making inroads against cancer and heart disease, two of the leading causes of death in the United States.

Although there is much to be proud of, medicine continues to face enormous challenges. Science has vanquished diseases such as smallpox and polio, but new killers, most notably AIDS, confront us. Moreover, we now victimize ourselves with what some have called "diseases of choice," or those brought on by drug and alcohol abuse, bad eating habits, and mismanagement of the stresses and strains of contemporary life. The very technology that is doing so much to prolong life has brought with it previously unimaginable ethical dilemmas related to issues of death and dying. The rising cost of health care is a matter of central concern to us all. And violence in the form of automobile accidents, homicide, and suicide remains the major killer of young adults.

In the past, most people were content to leave health care and medical treatment in the hands of professionals. But since the 1960s, the consumer of medical care—that is, the patient—has assumed an increasingly central role in the management of his or her own health. There has also been a new emphasis placed on prevention: People are recognizing that their own actions can help prevent many of the conditions that have caused death and disease in the past. This accounts for the growing commitment to good nutrition and regular exercise, for the increasing number of people who are choosing not to smoke, and for a new moderation in people's drinking habits.

People want to know more about themselves and their own health. They are curious about their body: its anatomy, physiology, and biochemistry. They want to keep up with rapidly evolving medical technologies and procedures. They are willing to educate themselves about common disorders and diseases so that they can be full partners in their own health care.

THE ENCYCLOPEDIA OF HEALTH is designed to provide the basic knowledge that readers will need if they are to take significant responsibility for their own health. It is also meant to serve as a frame of reference for further study and exploration. The encyclopedia is divided into five subsections: The Healthy Body; The Life Cycle; Medical Disorders & Their Treatment; Psychological Disorders & Their Treatment; and Medical Issues. For each topic covered by the encyclopedia, we present the essential facts about the relevant biology; the symptoms, diagnosis, and treatment of common diseases and disorders; and ways in which you can prevent or reduce the severity of health problems when that is possible. The encyclopedia also projects what may lie ahead in the way of future treatment or prevention strategies.

The broad range of topics and issues covered in the encyclopedia reflects that human health encompasses physical, psychological, social, environmental, and spiritual well-being. Just as the mind and the body are inextricably linked, so, too, is the individual an integral part of the wider world that comprises his or her family, society, and environment. To discuss health in its broadest aspect it is necessary to explore the many ways in which it is connected to such fields as law, social science, public policy, economics, and even religion. And so, the encyclopedia is meant to be a bridge between science, medical technology, the world at large, and you. I hope that it will inspire you to pursue in greater depth particular areas of interest and that you will take advantage of the suggestions for further reading and the lists of resources and organizations that can provide additional information.

CHAPTER 1

OUT OF THE DARKNESS

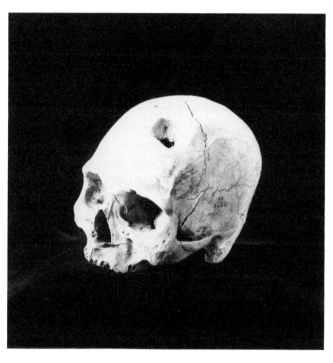

A skull with a trephine hole. Tribal healers may have used trephining as early as 4000 B.C. in attempts to treat mental retardation.

Throughout history, the issue of *mental retardation* has been a dark one, filled with gross injustices, misconceptions, and sometimes indescribable cruelty and violence. Before the dawn of recorded history, when survival of the fittest was a rule of life, it is unlikely that any mentally handicapped people survived. Life was harsh, and each member of a tribe or group was expected to pull his or her own weight by either gathering or hunting food. Comforts were few, and though it is certain that shamans, or religious leaders, often had a store of herbal remedies for illnesses, those who became sick or needed medical attention beyond the group's understanding usually died. Many cultures practiced infanticide, killing unwanted, deformed, or female offspring. In fact, in many places infanticide was not outlawed until the rise of Christianity, and even then was still practiced in outlying or rural areas. In cultures that believed in the survival of only the strongest or best specimens of humanity, it is probable that infants with physical deformities or noticeable mental handicaps were put to death. By contrast, the mildly retarded, who were simply a bit slower than normal, were probably accepted as long as their physical looks were pleasing.

Thus it was that most early cultures did not attempt to treat retardation, but rather sought to eliminate any trace of it. Nevertheless, there is evidence that in the Neolithic period, as early as 4000 B.C., shamans may have used *trephination* in attempts to treat persons with mental retardation and mental illness. The process of trephination involved cutting a hole in the sufferer's skull and removing a portion of the bone in order to allow the escape of evil spirits believed to be afflicting the person. Although it is doubtful that this crude surgery helped any of the sufferers, some did survive and lived for years afterward.

With the beginning of recorded history, many people surely commented or wrote about the mentally retarded, but most of their words and theories have been lost. In the 1st century A.D., the Roman aristocrat Celsus recommended that the severely retarded be treated with starvation, beating, and imprisonment. An Arab scholar of the ninth century, El Kendy, is believed to have been interested in mentally deficient people, but most early cultures grouped the mentally retarded, insane persons, and epileptics together into a single category. Because of this lack of differentiation, there was little clear understanding of mental retardation as a distinct entity.

Various cultures understood mental retardation differently. Many believed that it was a *hereditary* problem, resulting from the inferior match of marriage partners. In the face of some of the other causes suggested for retardation, however, heredity seems fairly reasonable.

During the Inquisition, thousands of people who were considered to be heretics were put to death. Many of them were believed to be witches possessed by demonic spirits. The beginning of the 11th century saw "witches" being burned at the stake throughout Europe. In the fervor of witch-hunting, anyone who was thought to be different— including the mentally ill, the epileptic, and the mentally retarded— was tried and put to death. They were judged to be evil or cohorts of the devil, although in fact they suffered from disease. Many died during these so-called witch-hunts, completely innocent and probably understanding very little of the reasoning for what happened to them. These witch-hunts did not stop until the end of the 18th century. Even Martin Luther, who was responsible for the Protestant Reformation of the 16th century, and who is still considered a great religious leader, had no sympathy for the mentally retarded. A believer in witches and demons, Luther felt that the retarded were at worst changelings brought under the influence of the devil, or were at best simply lumps of flesh. One of his suggested methods for treating the retarded was drowning them.

In the 13th century, King Edward II of England put into effect one of the first laws concerning retarded persons. His law decreed that the estates of mentally retarded persons would be held by the king during such persons' lifetimes, with all revenues from these estates coming to the king during those years. After each such person's death, the estate was returned in full to the family.

This law clearly had flaws. The families of retarded persons were usually reluctant to part with their estates, and therefore had their relatives ruled mentally ill instead. With such a ruling, the families of mentally ill persons were allowed to take over the running of their estates, and in doing so could reap all of the profits. Another problem with the law was the question of who really benefited. Although it was meant to protect the estates of retarded persons from those who would plunder them, the law was useful only to the wealthy and did nothing to protect the poor who were retarded and in much greater need of protection.

Before the end of the 19th century, mentally retarded persons were kept in institutions, where those who were considered disruptive were kept in chains or restraining cells such as this.

Poorer retarded people were often thrown into institutions with the mentally ill. This practice continued for centuries in one form or another. Such institutions were unsanitary at best. Inmates were often left to sit in their own wastes, made to sleep five or six in a bed, and offered little or no medical care. They were fed little and starved if they were uncooperative. Disruptive patients were kept chained in dank, dark rooms that were little more than dungeons. Beating was an accepted form of discipline.

Many of the "retarded" persons in these institutions were probably only mildly handicapped. Those who escaped were generally tolerated by the towns they lived in. These so-called "village idiots" were treated as objects of scorn and amusement but probably fared much better than those living in institutions. In many cases they were felt to be the responsibility of the town in which they lived, and the townspeople often gave them bits of food to eat or a place to stay.

For the most part, however, the retarded were treated most poorly, even by those who one would think ought to have known better. In fact, Pope Leo X was known to give large, elaborate parties at which dwarves and retarded persons were made the butts of cruel jokes or were even tormented physically for the guests' amusement.

SOME PROGRESS IS MADE

During the Middle Ages, the church and the state had both begun supporting abandoned or ill children. Instead of being killed, as they had been in earlier centuries, these children were placed in orphanages or foundling homes. Nevertheless, their fate was not much better than it had been before—in some places nearly 90% died while in these homes.

In the 16th century, the Swiss physician Aureolus Theophrastus Bombastus Von Hohenheim (1493–1541), known as Paracelsus, was the first to make the distinction between mental retardation and mental illness. He also noted that *cretinism*, caused by an underactive *thyroid gland*, was associated with mental retardation. In 1621, the Italian physician Tassoni introduced a new concept of mental retardation. Unlike many of his contemporaries, he believed that it was not heredity alone that caused retardation, but rather an excess of sensuality.

Also in the 1600s, Thomas Willis, known for his work with the circulatory system, included in his book *De Anima Brutorum* a chapter on mental deficiencies. Willis believed that stupidity, as he called it, was a result of excessive moisture or coldness in the brain. His recommended course of therapy included medicine to cleanse the blood, and the then-popular treatments of bleeding and purging to purify the body and mind.

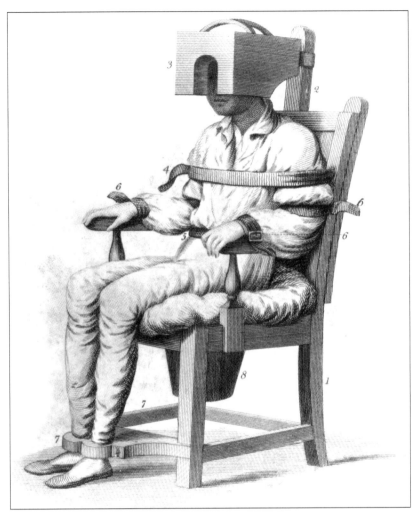

Before the advent of modern psychology, devices such as this tranquilizing chair were among the various means used for managing the mentally retarded.

Although Swiss physician Felix Platter (1536–1614) had already noted the existence of cretinism, Wolfgang Hoefer (1614–1681), a court physician in Vienna, offered the first extensive description of this condition in his book *Hercules Medicus, Sive Locorum Communium Medicorum Tomus Unicus*, published in 1657. If left untreated, the

Felix Platter, the Swiss physician who investigated cretinism.

condition, also known as *hypothyroidism*, results in a thickening of the lips, and protrusion of the tongue, low forehead, and stunted stature—the physical image of a cretin. Although Hoefer accurately described the condition, he mistakenly believed that it was caused by feeding a child too much bulky, fibrous food, and by inadequate education.

One of the first persons to advocate the humane treatment of the retarded was the French priest, Vincent de Paul (1581–1660). His early life of poverty and forced enslavement in Africa led de Paul to the belief that Christians had a responsibility to care for the mentally retarded and mentally ill. As a result, de Paul started charitable organizations dedicated to their cause. Among them were the Confraternity of Charity and the Daughters of Charity.

In 1632, de Paul was assigned to take over the Parisian priory of Saint-Lazure. Previously a home for lepers, the priory under de Paul also became a hospice for the mentally ill and the retarded. In later years, the priory was to become the Bicetre, one of the most famous institutions for the care of the mentally ill and retarded. In 1793, Philipe Pinel, a French physician, took over as head physician at the Bicetre. Appalled by the poor conditions of the patients and the physical abuse they suffered, Pinel instituted a policy of no physical abuse, and allowed patients to read books and to listen to music. Those who were judged capable were also trained in farming.

Pinel was perhaps the first administrator of an institution to propose humane treatment and even vocational training for the retarded. As such, he cleared a path for the better treatment of the retarded by those who followed him. Pinel was also well known for his work on classifying mental retardation. His book *A Treatise on Insanity*, published in 1801, listed what Pinel believed to be the classifications of mental retardation. Pinel's five categories of mental retardation included: (1) *melancholia* or delirium; (2) mania without delirium; (3) mania with delirium; (4) dementia, or abolition of the facility for thought; and (5) idiotism, or obliteration of the intellectual faculties and affections.

Among those who followed Pinel's footsteps in treating the retarded was William Tuke. Tuke and the Society of Friends, better known as the Quakers, established a hospital for the care of the retarded

Vincent de Paul, founder of the first permanent asylum in France for mentally disturbed children.

and insane in 1792. It was run according to Tuke's instructions, which provided for the kind and gentle treatment of its inhabitants.

Another follower of Pinel who was to make a name for himself in the field was one of his students, Jean-Marc-Gaspard Itard (1774–1838). A physician like Pinel, Itard worked at the National Institute for

Deaf Mutes. In 1797, an event took place that would alter the course of his life and secure him a place in history.

During that year, peasants living near a forest in France reported that they had seen a young boy running wild in the woods for some time. In 1798, the boy was captured and put on display. He escaped, however, and was not recaptured until the following year. Upon his recapture, the boy promptly escaped again and found his way to an

The French physician Philipe Pinel (1745–1826) was among the first to propose humane treatment for the mentally retarded — protection from physical abuse, permission to read books and listen to music, and provisions for vocational training for some followed.

official's office in Aveyron. Dubbed the "Wild Boy of Aveyron," he appeared to be severely retarded and desperate to escape.

Itard was hired to work with the boy, whom he described as being about 12 years old, a deaf mute, and pleasant looking. Itard worked with the boy for the next five years, hiring a housekeeper to live with him and giving him lessons. He named the boy Victor because he seemed to respond best to words with the O sound. Itard believed not that the boy had been born retarded but that living in the wild had prevented him from developing those faculties needed in a social environment. Therefore, he required help in developing his sensory, intellectual, and emotional abilities. Itard believed that with patience and education, the boy would make much progress.

Victor's case generated much attention. Because it was the first opportunity the medical community had had to study such a person, many prominent physicians of the time, including Pinel, wrote about him. Unlike Itard, however, Pinel believed that Victor was both mentally retarded and mentally ill, and could not be saved. After five years of training and personal attention, Itard was forced to end Victor's education. Although it was a difficult decision for him to make, Itard realized that the boy's progress had indeed been too slow, and that his problems were insurmountable. A housekeeper was hired to stay on with Victor, which she did, until he died a middle-aged man.

MAKING STRIDES

During the 19th century, John Langdon Down (1826–1896) was an English physician who served as superintendent of the Asylum for Idiots at Earlswood. Down is known best, however, for the condition that bears his name: *Down's syndrome.*

Down had his own theory of mental retardation. He believed that retardation fell into three categories: developmental, accidental, and *congenital.*

Congenital retardation, Down asserted, was an ethnic condition, in which the affected individuals bore certain similarities in appearance

A painting of Dr. Pinel freeing a mentally disturbed woman from her chains.

to certain ethnic population groups. Down devised a list of five types of such ethnic retardation: Ethiopian, Malay, Negroid, Aztec, and Mongolian. His theory was not widely accepted, however, since other physicians felt that retarded persons simply did not fit into these categories.

Nevertheless, the characteristics Down listed as typical of Mongolian retardation — thick lips, a broad face, and slanted eyes — did fit the description of one known form of retardation. Although widely

accepted as a type of cretinism, this retardation was actually the result of another condition, caused by an abnormality in the number of an individual's *chromosomes*. Eventually, this condition came to be called *mongolism*, after Down's classification of it. Today it is known as Down's syndrome.

After Down, another English physician, William Ireland (1832–1909), developed his own theories on the classification of mental retardation. In 1887, he published a comprehensive book on the subject, in which he proposed 10 classifications for retardation. Ireland's book also included information on education and legal matters related to the retarded.

It was the French physician Edouard Seguin (1812–1880), however, who was known to many as the father of special education for the retarded. Seguin, who had worked at the Bicetre in 1842, dedicated his life to helping the mentally retarded. He believed in both physical and sensory training for retarded children, and formed a private school for educating the retarded. He also practiced positive reinforcement of learned information, and encouraged his students to interact with their teachers. Seguin also tried to instill in the mentally retarded a sense of values and responsibility—a moral purpose.

In 1848, Seguin emigrated to the United States, where he was again to have a great impact on the education of the mentally retarded. In the United States, he helped start the Institution for Feeble-minded Youth in Barre, Massachusetts, and an experimental school in Albany, New York. After his second marriage, Seguin and his wife started the Seguin Physiological School for Feeble-minded Children in New York City. He was also instrumental in encouraging the establishment of the first association in America that was dedicated solely to the condition of mental retardation, the American Association on Mental Deficiency.

Swiss physician Johann Jakob Guggenbuhl (1816–1863), a contemporary of Seguin, also dedicated his life to the care of the retarded. In 1842, Guggenbuhl, who was interested in the cure and prevention of cretinism, opened the world's first residential facility for the mentally retarded at Abendberg, Switzerland, on land donated by a local forester. Guggenbuhl believed that the fresh mountain air, a good diet, and massage could cure cretinism and other forms of retardation.

Guggenbuhl ran his facility well. Patients were kept clean and given much attention. At first, physicians who toured the facility were greatly impressed with it, and word of Guggenbuhl's success spread throughout the European medical community. In the midst of this high reputation, Guggenbuhl left the facility to tour and talk about his theories. While gone, he left his stepfather in charge of the facility. It was to be his undoing. Guggenbuhl's stepfather let the conditions in the hospice deteriorate greatly: it became unsanitary and crowded, with inadequate food and supplies.

When word of these poor conditions began to spread, Guggenbuhl's reputation was tarnished. Those who visited the decaying facility spoke of how little progress had been made and how badly the patients were treated. Ultimately, Guggenbuhl was forced to close the facility. He never regained his reputation and died in 1863, a scorned man.

EDUCATIONAL IMPROVEMENTS

Another who was to make a mark in the field of education for the mentally retarded was the first Italian female physician, Maria Montessori (1870–1952). Working from a psychiatric clinic in Rome, Montessori toured asylums, and felt pity for the children she saw in them. In 1896, she decided to travel to London and Paris to study the theories of Itard and Seguin.

Montessori believed that children had an innate sense of dignity, preferred hard work to idleness, liked to make choices for themselves, and thrived on repetition. She further believed that teachers shouldn't "educate" so much as provide a fertile environment in which a child's own ideas could take root and grow. She believed that in such an environment, revelations would naturally come to the children, making education a more spontaneous process.

This spontaneous education process was the foundation of Montessori's unorthodox views. She worked personally with the children for whom she was responsible and was so successful that some of her students were able to pass tests at levels equal to those of ordinary children. Montessori eventually began to apply her principles to normal children, and she worked with them until the end of her life. Her schools became popular throughout the United States and Europe, and although not all of her ideas have stood the test of time, many of these schools remain in existence today.

The Swiss physician Paracelsus (1493–1541) was the first person to make the distinction between mental retardation and mental illness.

THE UNITED STATES TAKES CENTER STAGE

After completing his education at the Harvard Medical School, Samuel Gridley Howe (1801–1876) went on to work with blind children. In 1839, while director of the Perkins Institute and the Massachusetts School for the Blind, Howe accepted a blind, mentally retarded child for training. Having proved successful with this first student, Howe then began accepting other retarded pupils and was soon urging the U.S. government to create a private, residential facility for the care of the mentally retarded.

Howe's advocacy worked. In 1846, the U.S. House of Representatives appointed a three-member committee to look into the conditions of mentally retarded people in the United States and to recommend what the country should do for them. Howe was asked to be a member of the panel.

The committee members visited with mentally retarded individuals around the country and recommended that a school be formed for their education. Congress agreed in 1848 to finance a $2,500 experimental school for 10 mentally retarded children for a period of three years.

The school was opened in a wing of the Perkins Institute, and it was a success. Howe's work paved the way for the establishment of the Massachusetts School for Idiots and Feebleminded Youth in 1855. Howe remained dedicated to his students until the end of his life.

Although Howe's wing of the Perkins Institute was known as an experimental school for the mentally retarded, it was really more of a residential facility. It was not, however, the first private residential center for the mentally retarded in the United States. Such a center had been opened in Barre, Massachusetts, in 1848, under the administration of Dr. Hervey B. Wilbur (1820–1883).

Wilbur's involvement with the retarded began when he took into his home the young, retarded child of a lawyer who was an acquaintance of his. From this point onward, his interest in the mentally retarded grew—as did his involvement with them. In 1851 he left Barre to become superintendent of the Syracuse Institution for the Feeble-minded. In 1876, he helped found the Association of Medical Officers of American Institutions for Idiots and Feeble-minded Persons.

The Association was created to provide for a forum for discussion among professionals, with the goal of encouraging the establishment of more institutions for the treatment and education of the retarded. The Association even had its own publication. In 1907, the group changed its name to the American Association for the Study of the Feeble-minded, and in 1933 it became the American Association on Mental Deficiency.

Following the creation of both Howe and Wilbur's residential communities, other such facilities for the mentally retarded began to spring up in the United States. In 1852, a private residential facility was founded in Germantown, Pennsylvania. This facility later moved to Media, Pennsylvania, and became known as the Elwyn Institute. By 1898, there were 24 institutions for the mentally retarded in 19 states.

During the 1800s, the idea of vocational training for the mentally retarded also took hold in the United States. Many retarded individuals were able to work. Those with milder handicaps could perform regular work-related duties, while those with more severe handicaps could often perform repetitious activities. Some of the work programs that were set up at this time even allowed for a salary for participants. Unfortunately, however, many programs simply used the retarded as free labor.

During the late 19th century, the public took a lively interest in the welfare and education of children in the United States, and many laws were passed to try to improve their lot. Most of this legislation, however, purposely excluded retarded children. Nevertheless, it was at this time that the first public school classes for children in need of special education were created in the United States. These classes, and other educational developments, will be discussed in more detail in chapter 4.

The late 1800s also saw the wide adoption of the Colony Plan facility for housing and treating the retarded. This plan involved breaking a facility into four parts, consisting of a training school, an industrial department, a custodial department, and an agricultural department. Participants were placed in these departments according to their abilities and levels of functioning. In the United States, the Colony Plan persisted into the 20th century.

THE TWENTIETH CENTURY

The 20th century saw great strides in the field of mental retardation but also witnessed a few small steps backward.

Until the late 19th century, America's Barnum & Bailey Circus had featured "bird-headed" dwarves, who were really suffering from a type of retardation that includes a smaller-than-average size head. The circus also had Zip, the "Monkey Man." This person was actually a poor, black, retarded boy who was billed as a sort of missing link. Such exploitation of the retarded was not new, but as the twentieth century went on, it became rarer.

In 1906, Dr. Henry Goddard, who later became professor of clinical psychology at Ohio State University, was appointed director of the Vineland Training School in New Jersey where he set up the first American laboratory devoted to the study of mental retardation. Goddard was a great believer in the heredity theory of retardation. Many of his own theories were without validity, however, and most of his work is no longer accepted.

In 1909, an English physician, Archibald E. Garrod, published *Inborn Errors of Metabolism*, a book in which he put forth the theory that retardation was the result of a *genetic* abnormality. Garrod theorized that the abnormality produced the retardation by blocking crucial steps in the body's chemical processes. Ironically, although Garrod's theory was largely true, it was not widely accepted until the 1940s.

Another English physician, Eugene Talbot, also proved to be years ahead of his time when in 1911 he cautioned pregnant women to avoid alcohol, narcotics, and tobacco. In addition, Talbot also recognized that diseases such as scarlet fever and whooping cough, as well as malnutrition, could cause retardation, and he understood lead and mercury to be causative agents in the intellectual impairment of children.

By the early 1900s, 39 states in America had passed laws prohibiting marriage among mentally retarded persons, or had ruled that the marriage of a mentally retarded person could be annulled. Some states even forced prospective spouses to take an oath that they were not feebleminded. In many cases, however, such laws proved ineffective.

At the same time, a debate raged over the issue of the sterilization of mentally retarded adults. The argument for sterilization included the idea that it would allow mentally retarded persons to marry without the fear that they would produce offspring. In 1907, Indiana became the first state to pass a law allowing the sterilization of the mentally retarded. By 1912, seven other states had similar laws. Some states allowed the sterilization of rapists, criminals, epileptics, and insane persons. Iowa even permitted the sterilization of alcoholic persons, drug addicts, prostitutes, and persons suffering from *syphilis*.

By 1958, sterilization had been legalized in 30 states, and from 1900 to 1958, more than 30,000 such procedures were performed, mainly on women. Some states did not even require consent from the individual who was to be sterilized. Even for those retarded persons who lived in states that did require consent, however, there was little choice, since such persons were given only two options—sterilization or institutionalization.

With the passing of laws governing sterilization, various states began to authorize other laws concerning the mentally retarded. Some states prohibited the sale of alcohol to retarded individuals. Others prohibited them from owning or using firearms. Some states did not permit retarded persons to vote or serve in the National Guard. On a more positive note, 13 states had laws prohibiting the mistreatment of retarded adults, which protected them from use in freak shows and carnivals.

The 20th century also saw an increase in the number of retarded persons living in institutions. At the turn of the century, there had only been about 10,000 institutionalized mentally retarded people; thirty years later, the number was close to 70,000.

Among the few physicians who were greatly interested in the treatment of institutionalized retarded persons was Dr. Charles Bernstein (1872–1942). Bernstein believed that an institutional environment had an adverse effect on the development of retarded persons. Instead, he felt that they were best treated in settings more like those of normal families. Bernstein believed that facilities providing for such settings should be built so that the retarded could lead more ordinary lives. By 1935 more than 50 such group homes had been founded in the United States.

THE MENTALLY RETARDED AND THE MILITARY

Despite their handicaps, both real and perceived, mentally retarded persons served in World War I and did a credible job. Although draft boards were allowed to reject applicants who were believed to be retarded, many retarded persons with a normal appearance slipped through the process and got into the army.

After the war, the army adopted a rule that anyone at the mental age of eight years old would be permitted to serve. In World War II, as Hitler put thousands of mentally retarded people to death in an effort to form a perfect race, many mentally retarded people in the United States joined the armed forces. In addition, a mental age of ten was put forth as a requirement for the navy. As a result, thousands of retarded men joined up to fight. Even those retarded persons who did not go to war were not left out in the cold, since the shortage of able-bodied men opened up a host of job opportunities for other groups. Tragically, however, even those persons who had performed admirably in the war were sent back to institutions upon their return to the United States, since no nationwide vocational rehabilitation program was in effect.

MEDICAL ADVANCES

Much information about mental retardation was brought to light in the years prior to World War II. In 1924, Dr. Charles Davenport put forth the theory that Down's syndrome was caused by a chromosomal abnormality. In 1934, Norwegian scientist Ivar Folling identified *phenylketonuria*, or PKU, a *metabolic* disorder, which if left untreated could result in mental retardation. In 1939, George Jervis of New York's Letchworth Village—a state-run institution for the retarded—uncovered the tie between PKU and a deficiency in the body's ability to use the amino acid known as *phenylalanine*. In the first half of the century, scientists also began to note that most mothers of infants with Down's syndrome were considerably older than most mothers of normal infants.

Other progress quickly followed. In 1940, *Rh incompatability*—a condition that results when the blood type of a fetus contains a specific enzyme that is chemically different from the same enzyme in the blood of its mother—was first noted as a cause of mental retardation. Then in 1954, *maple syrup urine disease*, a metabolic disorder named for the smell it produces in the affected infant's urine, was first identified as a cause of retardation. Five years later, in 1959, Dr. Jerome Lejeune and his colleagues at the University of Paris discovered that people with Down's syndrome had 47 chromosomes instead of the normal human complement of 46. That same year the chromosomal abnormalities resulting in *Klinefelter's syndrome* and *Turner's syndrome* were also noted.

Still more progress was to come. In the early 1970s, Dr. Jean Dussault, a Canadian physician, devised a test to detect in infants the hypothyroidism that causes cretinism. To do this, he employed the then-new procedure of *radioimmunoassay*, in which thyroid deficiency could be determined by placing a small amount of an infant's blood, usually gotten through a simple heel prick, on a piece of filter paper.

In 1974, the province of Quebec set up a screening program for infantile hypothyroidism with Dussault in charge. The United States began screening in 1975, and by 1979, 12 European nations were screening for hypothyroidism. Soon after, Dr. Robert Guthrie of Buffalo was able to devise a test for PKU, also using radioimmunoassay. Today, most developed nations do screening for hypothyroidism, PKU, and a host of other conditions.

Today, more is known about mental retardation than was ever thought possible. In the early 1980s, scientists uncovered a new form of retardation, related to chromosome damage. Known as *fragile X syndrome*, it is believed to cause 5% to 10% of all mental retardation in the United States today.

OTHER ADVANCES

In the mid-20th century, parents began to take a more active role in the decisions made about their mentally retarded children. Parents' groups began springing up in local communities throughout the United States.

In 1950, some of these parents concluded that there was a need for a national organization consisting of and representing the parents of retarded children. Thus they created Parents and Friends of Mentally Retarded Children. In 1980 this became the Association for Retarded Citizens of the United States (ARC). It retains that name today, and has a membership consisting of hundreds of local chapters.

In 1953, the United States guaranteed that every retarded child has the right to a suitable education. This idea was reinforced and expanded upon by the Education for All Handicapped Children Act of 1975. During the 1960s, with the support of President John F. Kennedy, the government took a special interest in the mentally retarded. Kennedy, who had a retarded sister, formed the President's Panel on Mental Retardation in 1961, charging the panel with the research and recommendation of care and programs for the retarded. Special funding programs for the retarded were also put into effect under the Kennedy administration, including social security benefits. Additionally, the number of professional training programs for the retarded increased, as did the number of positions open to retarded adults.

When during the 1970s conditions at institutions for the retarded were found to be poorer than had been thought, a federal *deinstitutionalization* plan was suggested. Although parents of past generations had been discouraged from bringing their retarded infants home, doctors now recommended that such children be raised by their own families.

Although persons with mental handicaps are better treated today than at any other time in American history, the discovery that their child is retarded remains one of life's most painful and problematic experiences for parents. Chapter 2 will discuss this this age-old problem more closely, and take a look at some of the causes of mental retardation.

CHAPTER 2

WHAT CAUSES RETARDATION?

Although children with Down's syndrome typically experience mental retardation, its severity may vary widely, with some affected children able to read, complete their schooling, and lead nearly normal lives.

In the bed lies a new mother, contented, smiling, and relaxing after the long birth of her son, and dreaming of her baby's first smile, his first step, and the first time he calls her "Mama." Her dreams are shattered when a doctor comes and tells her that her baby is retarded. To some parents the news comes later. They have a seemingly perfect baby, who rarely cries and is content to stay in her crib — and who never smiles, does not seem to care whether anyone holds her or not, and has shown no interest in trying to crawl. In fact, she doesn't seem to have the ability, although other babies at this age that the parents know seem to be crawling. The parents talk to their pediatrician, who recommends that the infant be tested. The results show that the child is retarded.

A LIFE SENTENCE

For parents, the news that a child is retarded is typically a nightmare. It requires that they take on the difficult task of replanning their lives to include a mentally retarded child who will need lifelong help.

Although once many parents simply left their retarded children in hospitals and never looked back, this is certainly not the case today. For example, in a recent survey, 9 out of 10 families of children with Down's syndrome born in Manchester, England, took these children home with them.

This is not to say that the decision to keep retarded children at home is an easy one. The Manchester survey also found that 70% to 80% of the mothers of the affected children admitted to having feelings of rejection toward their children in the first few months after they were born.

Parents of retarded children experience a wide range of emotions, which resemble those felt in the normal grieving process. First, there is denial of the fact that the baby is retarded. Next come feelings of depression and of being unable to continue life with such a burden. Feelings of hopelessness and helplessness follow. There is often also anger and guilt. The parents' anger can be directed at themselves, family members, medical personnel, or the child. Many mothers of retarded children feel guilty about being angry with their children, or about sometimes being unable to love them. A parent may also feel guilty for believing that something he or she did caused the child's handicap.

A period of bargaining with God or trying a variety of doctors in a quest for miracle cures may follow this first phase. At this stage, many parents are vulnerable to charlatans who may promise quick cures for large sums of money. When the remedies fail, the parents' hopes are dashed.

In most cases, the parents eventually enter into a period of adjustment during which they realistically prepare for the care of their new child and set goals for the future. This period of adjustment is naturally much easier if the parents have had prior knowledge of the child's handicap as a result of *prenatal testing*. In any case, for most parents, after finding out their child is retarded the first question asked is: How could this have happened?

THE ORIGINS OF MENTAL RETARDATION

Mental retardation can be caused by a number of factors. Most of the causes, however, can be categorized as either chromosomal, metabolic, or environmental.

Chromosomal Sources of Retardation

To understand the chromosomal abnormalities that cause mental retardation, it is first necessary to have a basic understanding of chromosomes and the part they play in heredity.

Most children share certain physical features with their parents. The genetic information that determines whether a baby will have its mother's blue eyes or its father's brown ones, or if the infant will have the red hair that runs on one side of the family, is found in the rod-shaped structures known as chromosomes, which carry the genetic material of each parent. Specifically, this genetic information is carried in the subunits of chromosomes that are known as genes, where it is encoded in the material known as deoxyribonucleic acid, or DNA.

When a child is conceived, the fertilization of the mother's egg cell, or ovum, by one of the father's sperm cells normally gives the resulting

The English physician John Langdon Down (1828–1896), who believed that mental retardation fell into five categories based on the physical characteristics of affected individuals. One of his categories came to be applied to the condition now known as Down's syndrome, or trisomy 21.

zygote—the earliest stage of the embryo—a full complement of 46 chromosomes. As the fertilized egg begins to duplicate and divide, the parents' genetic information is passed along to each new cell.

Each of the parents' sex cells, the ovum and the sperm cell, carries 23 of these 46 chromosomes. Each chromosome in the mother's egg cell is matched by one that corresponds in both size and shape to it in the father's sperm cell. Of the 46 chromosomes, or 23 pairs, 22 of the pairs are chromosomes responsible for a variety of different traits and functions. The sole exception is the last pair, or set, of chromosomes, which is responsible for determining the sex of the developing infant.

The female sex chromosome resembles the letter X, while the male sex chromosome more closely resembles the letter Y. If the coming together of the sperm and egg produces a cell with two *X chromosomes*, the resulting child will be female. If, on the other hand, the union of the two sex cells results in a fertilized zygote that has both an X and a *Y chromosome*, the child will be male.

In the case of Down's syndrome, the cluster of symptoms and effects that include mental retardation results from an additional chromosome in the 21st set of human chromosomes. Consequently, the scientific name for the disease is trisomy 21, meaning that there are three (tri) chromosomes instead of the usual two in the 21st set of chromosomes.

Other *trisomies* causing retardation are trisomy 13 and trisomy 18. Trisomy 13, or Patau's syndrome, is caused by the presence of 3 number 13 chromosomes. It occurs in less then 1 out of every 2,000 live births, and can cause a smaller-than-average head, small eyes or an absence of eyes, cleft lips and a cleft palate, low-set ears, heart defects, and abnormal genitalia, as well as severe retardation. Most persons with this syndrome do not survive past childhood.

Trisomy 18, in which there are 3 rather than 2 of the number 18 chromosomes, occurs even less frequently than trisomy 13, affecting less than 1 out of every 4,000 live births. It too can cause small head size, low-set ears, smaller-than-average jaws, heart defects, and mis-shapen fingers and toes, in addition to severe retardation. Most of those affected with this disease also do not survive beyond infancy.

Diagnosing Down's Syndrome

The diagnosis of Down's syndrome is usually made right after the birth of a child, since infants with the syndrome show several significant physical differences from the average baby.

One of these differences is slanting eyes, often with heavy-looking eyelids, that once led the disease to be known as mongolism, as discussed in chapter 1. This slant is caused by an additional fold in the eyelid at the inner corner of the eye. The heads of infants with Down's syndrome are also flatter than normal, and their necks are shorter, with a pad of fat at the back. Affected infants often have little or no muscle tone, and in some cases, instead of the normal three creases on the palm of the hand, there is a horizontal crease known as the simian line.

Other physical characteristics of the syndrome can include white specks in the iris, or colored part of the eye, low ears, and protrusion of the tongue resulting from a smaller-than-average mouth. An absence of the 12th rib is noted in some cases, as well as are other abnormalities of the skeletal system, including a small pelvis.

A child with Down's syndrome being given a roller-cart ride at a camp for handicapped children. The appearance of the eyes of persons with the syndrome is a genetic effect, caused by the development of an epicanthic fold in the eyelid at the inner corner of the eye.

Further physical abnormalities in some children with Down's syndrome include heart defects and problems involving the immune system. In addition to this, children with Down's syndrome often have brains that are smaller than average, although this alone does not account for retardation. However, the smaller-than-average size of the brain stem and cerebellum in children with the syndrome may explain why many of those affected by it have trouble with coordination, since these parts of the brain control many basic body functions.

The degree of mental retardation caused by Down's syndrome ranges widely, from very minor in highly functioning people like actor Chris Burke on the television series "Life Goes On" to so severe that the intelligence level is kept to that of a toddler. The majority of people with Down's syndrome, however, have mild to moderate retardation, meaning that they will be slow to walk and speak, but will eventually be able to read. Many hold jobs, and some even live on their own.

Down's Syndrome and Maternal Age

Scientists still have little understanding about why the number of children born with Down's syndrome grows dramatically as the age of the mother increases. According to a 1988 report, approximately 1 out of every 800 to 1,000 infants born in the United States has Down's syndrome, whereas the number rises to 38 per 1,000 births for mothers who are 46 years old and older.

Whatever the reason for the increased rate of birth of Down's syndrome infants among older women, physicians recommend that *amniocentesis* or *chorionic villi sampling* (see sidebar), be done in mothers 35 years of age and older, since these tests can reassure parents that their fetus is normal or provide them with information they will require to accommodate an infant who has special needs.

The life expectancy for children with Down's syndrome has risen dramatically in the last century. In 1930, the life expectancy for a child with Down's syndrome was only nine years. Today, although nearly 15% of children with the syndrome die before the age of five years, largely from such physical problems as heart defects, most of the remaining children have the same chance of reaching age 40 as other children their age. After age 40, the number of deaths among persons with Down's syndrome is some 30 percent higher than normal.

Turner and Klinefelter's syndromes are two conditions that result from an abnormality in the chromosomes. Neither condition necessarily results in mental retardation, and even when this does occur, the handicap is usually mild.

Turner's syndrome is the result of an infant either having only a single X chromosome rather than the two that are typical in female infants, or having one defective and one normal X chromosome. It occurs only in female infants, at a rate of approximately one in every 3,000 births. Its characteristics can include a webbed neck, low hairline, smaller than average height, and heart and kidney problems. Women with Turner's syndrome are also sterile.

Klinefelter's syndrome affects approximately one of every 1,000 male newborns. It is caused by the presence of two X and one Y chromosome, and like Turner's syndrome, also causes sterility. Because they have male genitalia, children with Klinefelter's syndrome are often not identified until puberty, when their breast tissue frequently becomes enlarged.

Discovered in the early 1980s, fragile X syndrome is the most recently identified chromosomal abnormality to be known as a cause of retardation among newborns, and may be the leading cause of inherited retardation. It results from a weakness in the X chromosome, and more often affects males—who have only one X chromosome— than females. Since all females have two X chromosomes, those who inherit the weakened X chromosome can often make up for it with a healthy second X chromosome.

Despite this, many male infants who inherit the fragile X chromosome are unaffected by the syndrome, and not all female infants escape it. According to a 1987 report, nearly 80% of male carriers of the chromosome are retarded, and two-thirds of its female carriers are not. Scientists have not been able to uncover the reason for this.

A young boy who is retarded gets some help from a special education teacher in how to fold clothes.

In 1986, geneticist W. Ted Brown of the New York State Institute for Basic Research in Developmental Disabilities created a test for identifying fragile X syndrome. In this test, small portions of genetic material, recovered by amniocentesis, are removed from a few cells of a fetus that is thought to have the syndrome, and are compared to similar material taken from relatives who do not have the condition. This testing cannot, however, ascertain whether the fetus will be retarded or not. As already noted, carriers of the fragile X syndrome can remain unaffected by it. The condition can, however, show up in later generations.

In a study reported in February 1991, French scientist Jean-Louis Mandel of Strasbourg University and his colleagues at both the university and the Pasteur Institute in Paris discovered that parts of the genes of persons with the fragile X syndrome were shut down, and did not function. This theory had been proposed by Charles Laird of the University of Washington at Seattle. Laird had noted that one of the two X chromosomes in every cell of a woman's body is normally inactivated. However, it is turned on once again at the time of reproduction, and enters into her offspring.

Laird theorized that the abnormality in the fragile X chromosome prevents some of the genes in the activated X chromosome from being turned on once again during reproduction, and that when this pattern is passed along to a future generation, the syndrome could surface once again.

Scientists are still studying the fragile X syndrome, and much remains to be learned about it. It is currently recommended that any person suffering from unexplained retardation be tested for the syndrome, since this can help pinpoint the risk of its occurrence in other relatives.

Although it is possible for a person to have an extra chromosome, as in Down's syndrome, it is not possible for an infant to survive with only 45 chromosomes, and such defects are probably responsible for the many miscarriages recorded each year. It is possible, however, for an infant to survive with only a portion of a chromosome. Such conditions are known as *deletion abnormalities*. They occur during cell division and usually result in an infant with 45 chromosomes plus a fraction of the forty-sixth chromosome.

The actor and comedian Jack Klugman poses with a group of
people of various ages who suffer from Down's syndrome. During the
past half-century, the survival rate of persons with Down's syndrome
has increased sharply, so that it is now the same as the national
average until the age of 40 years.

One such abnormality results in the condition known as *cri du chat syndrome*, named for the catlike cry made by infants afflicted with it. Caused by the absence of a portion of the number five chromosome, the *cri du chat* syndrome also results in a small head and slanted, wide-set eyes. Another deletion abnormality occurs when a portion of chromosome number 18 is missing. This condition results in mental retardation, seizures, heart defects, and other problems.

Besides abnormal chromosome additions and deletions, there is another type of chromosomal abnormality that causes mental retardation called a *translocation abnormality*. This occurs when a portion of one chromosome is somehow removed and transferred to another chromosome where it does not belong. One condition that can result from such an abnormality is *translocation Down's syndrome*.

The carrier for this condition is a parent who does not suffer from the condition but instead has 46 chromosomes and functions normally. One of the parent's number 21 chromosomes, however, is attached to either the number 14 or the number 15 pair of chromosomes. When the parent's egg or sperm cell produces a zygote, the genetic code for the translocated number 21 chromosome may be passed on to the zygote. The union with the other parent's sex cell, with its normal complement of 23 chromosomes, will therefore result in an infant with 47 chromosomes. This child is then said to be an unbalanced translocation carrier and will be affected by Down's syndrome. Fortunately, the retardation in translocation Down's syndrome is usually mild.

CHAPTER 3
METABOLIC AND ENVIRONMENTAL CAUSES

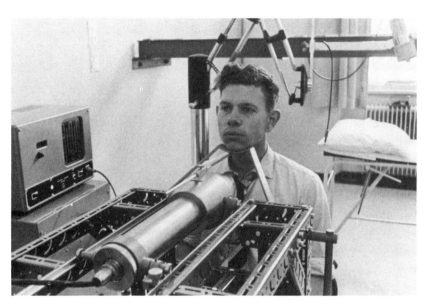

The low functioning of the thyroid gland known as hypothyroidism can cause severe mental retardation in the infant of a woman who does not ingest an adequate quantity of iodine or has other problems affecting her thyroid gland during pregnancy. The thyroid function of this teenage boy is being measured with a device that determines the extent to which a special radioactive substance gathers in the thyroid gland.

In addition to chromosomal abnormalities, retardation can be caused by a number of other conditions, among them metabolic abnormalities that occur within the body's chemical processes.

The human body produces tens of thousands of substances that ensure that its organs and cells function normally. If even one of these substances is not produced or is produced in an aberrant form, the delicate balance of the body's functioning is thrown off, and retardation can occur.

Phenylketonuria, or PKU, already discussed in chapter 1, is one such condition. It results when the body lacks the enzyme known as phenylalanine hydroxylase, which is normally produced by the liver. This enzyme helps to transform phenylalanine—one of the amino acids needed for the building of protein—into tyrosine, another substance, some of which is excreted, and some of which is used by the body.

Because lack of the enzyme prevents phenylalanine from being normally transformed or broken down, the amino acid accumulates in the bloodstream of persons with PKU and can damage brain tissue, causing retardation. The body's failure to transform phenylalanine into tyrosine also leads to a fair-skinned, light-eyed, and light-haired person, since tyrosine is needed for creating the pigments that give hair, eyes, and freckles their color. Fortunately, it occurs in only 1 out of every 10,000 births.

PKU cannot be detected by amniocentesis or other such methods, but procedures to screen for the disease are now available. These procedures can detect PKU by the third day after birth or following two full days of feeding. If the condition is found early, and the affected infant is given a special diet lacking phenylalanine, brain damage can be avoided.

Another metabolic disorder responsible for mental retardation is maple syrup urine disease. Rare and hereditary, this disease also involves a problem with the metabolic transformation of amino acids. Rather than involving a single amino acid as does PKU, however, it involves four amino acids and a single enzyme that converts all of them into other substances.

At birth and for a while thereafter, the infant with maple syrup urine disease will appear to be fine. The baby will, however, eventually develop feeding problems, lose the normal startle reflex, and develop an irregular breathing pattern. These problems persist and are later joined by muscular rigidity and convulsions. As the name of the disease implies, infants affected by it excrete urine that has a sweet odor similar to that of maple syrup. Affected infants can die in the first few weeks

Because You Love Your Baby...

QUIT SMOKING DURING PREGNANCY

AMERICAN ≡ LUNG ASSOCIATION
The Christmas Seal People®

A poster from the American Lung Association advises mothers that smoking may harm unborn children. Smoking can be a factor in the mental retardation of offspring.

of life. If the disease is diagnosed in the first day or two of life, an affected infant can be given a special diet, as in PKU, and retardation can be avoided.

In *galactosemia*, the substance that gathers in abnormal quantities in the blood and urine is not an amino acid, as in PKU or maple syrup urine disease, but the sugar *galactose*. The most common cause of galactosemia is a deficiency of the enzyme galactose-1-phosphate uridyltransferase, which works in the liver to convert lactose, the sugar found in milk, into galactose and another sugar, glucose. Glucose, a simple sugar, can be used by the body as fuel, but galactose must be further broken down into glucose before it can be utilized. Without the enzyme, this is not possible, and the galactose builds up in the bloodstream, destroying cells and spilling over into the urine.

The symptoms of galactosemia come upon an affected infant rapidly, regardless of the type of nutrition he or she is receiving. They include lethargy, diarrhea, vomiting, jaundice (a yellowish cast to the skin and the whites of the eyes, caused by the buildup of another liver enzyme in the body), cataracts (a milky white film covering the eye), and enlargement of the liver. If left untreated, the disease can cause retardation and even death by the third day after birth. Infants who do survive without treatment have cataracts and become mentally retarded. Once again, however, with an early diagnosis the child is given a special diet, in this case one free of galactose, to prevent damage, although any already existing effects of the disease cannot be reversed.

Like the other diseases described above, untreated hypothyroidism can also produce retardation, as noted in chapter 1. However, the particular type of retardation caused by hypothyroidism is one of the most difficult for both parents and doctors to cope with.

The thyroid gland is part of the body's system of endocrine glands, which exercise control over various aspects of sexual function, metabolism, and other vital bodily activities. The thyroid gland has two parts, called lobes, located on either side of the trachea in the front of the neck. The glands of the endocrine system exert their control over various body processes by producing hormones, substances that they secrete into the bloodstream. The bloodstream then carries them to the target organs over which they exert their control.

Hypothyroidism can be caused by a mother's inadequate intake of iodine during pregnancy, or by a low level of thyroid function. Infants who have the condition as a result of such maternal deficiencies, and who are not treated, develop cretinism.

Cretinism, as discussed in chapter 1, is a condition marked by severe retardation and digestive problems, as well as stunted growth, a thick and protruding tongue, arms and legs that are abnormally short, and coarse features, giving these people a dwarflike appearance.

The most tragic aspect of hypothyroidism is that infants born with the disease appear perfectly normal, but by the time symptoms begin to appear, they have already experienced irreversible brain damage that has caused retardation. This is because the hormones produced by the thyroid gland are essential to growth, and without them brain cells, which grow most rapidly in the first few months following birth, are unable to develop properly. Fortunately, a simple screening process is available to prenatally detect hypothyroidism, which occurs in 1 out of every 4,000 live births.

Two other abnormalities responsible for mental retardation are *hydrocephalus* and *cerebral palsy*. In hydrocephalus, spinal fluid builds up in the brain, causing enlargement of the head and bulging of the forehead, with damage to brain tissue. Cerebral palsy is an almost catchall term for a number of conditions ranging from physical injury to problems at birth, many of which are accompanied by retardation. On the other hand, many children with cerebral palsy do retain their intellectual capacity despite their having problems with nerve damage and muscle control.

Also responsible for some cases of retardation is an incompatibility between the blood type of a mother and her fetus. The blood type of any individual is determined by a complex set of protein substances that exist on the individual's blood cells and are passed along to that person's offspring via genetic mechanisms. Of the four main blood types—A, B, AB, and O—the most common is type O. Each blood type may also be positive or negative. Most persons are of positive blood

Dr. Harry Meyer, Jr., and Dr. Paul Parkman of the U.S. National In-
stitutes of Health in Bethesda, Maryland, developed a vaccine that
has proven widely effective in preventing rubella. However, despite
the now customary practice of rubella vaccination during childhood,
as many as 15% of women may reach childbearing age without
having been vaccinated.

type, meaning that their blood cells contain a protein known as the *Rh*
factor. Blood types that do not have the Rh factor are designated Rh
negative, and are represented as A-, or O-, for example, as opposed to
A+ or O+. Negative blood types are much rarer than positive blood
types.

When a mother with an Rh-negative blood type becomes pregnant
with a fetus that has an Rh-positive blood type, problems arise. The

mother's body, sensing something inside itself that is foreign (the baby's blood, which contains a protein substance that her own blood lacks), takes steps to attack and destroy the foreign material. Fortunately for the child, there is little or no exchange of blood between a mother and her fetus during pregnancy. When such an exchange does occur, however, the mother's body reacts by killing red blood cells in the fetus. This in turn can deprive the fetus of oxygen, which can lead to retardation.

If the mother's blood and that of her fetus are commingled either before or at birth, the mother's body also begins to build up an arsenal of more permanent weapons to fight the alien Rh-positive cells should they ever again appear in her body. These weapons are produced by her immune system and are known as antibodies. If the mother then has a second child with an Rh-positive blood type, that child's blood has a much greater chance of being attacked by these maternal antibodies.

Fortunately, a substance known as RhoGAM, derived from the immune system, can today be used to counteract the maternal antibodies that occur in Rh incompatibility. If given to the mother shortly after the birth of her first Rh-positive infant, it can assure that each new fetus will have an equal chance of surviving within her uterus until it is born.

MATERNAL HEALTH AND RETARDATION

Contrary to widespread belief, most cases of mental retardation in the United States today do not come from the causes that have so far been discussed in this book. Among the genetic causes of retardation, it is true that Down's syndrome is the most common and perhaps the most visible to the public. However, recent attention in the media has given Down's syndrome much exposure, and may have made it seem responsible for many more cases of retardation than it actually is.

The past saw many cases of retardation that could not be explained; the discovery of fragile X syndrome has provided an explanation for many of these cases. What most people do not realize, however, is that nearly half of all cases of retardation come from disease-causing germs and other agents that are acquired—and not inherited—by pregnant

PRENATAL TESTING

Although there are several methods of prenatal testing—including sonograms—there are basically two that can inform parents about chromosomal abnormalities that lead to mental retardation. These two tests are amniocentesis and sampling of the chorionic villi (CVS).

Amniocentesis is performed between the 14th and 16th weeks of gestation. (A normal gestation lasts from 38 to 40 weeks, or approximately nine months). Before amniocentesis is done, a sonograph (an image-making procedure similar to an X ray) is taken to locate the placenta—the structure to which the fetus is attached and through which it derives its nutrients. The mother's abdomen is then anesthetized so that she will not experience any discomfort, and a thin needle is inserted through her abdomen and into her uterus. Amniotic fluid is then withdrawn through the needle.

The amniotic fluid contains skin cells that have sloughed off during the fetus's growth. These cells can be used to determine a fetal karyotype—a type of photograph of a fetus's chromosomes. Amniocentesis is recommended for women who have or may have certain genetic diseases, those who are experiencing problems in their pregnancy, and those who are over 35 years of age. The test is recommended for older women mainly because the incidence of Down's syndrome increases greatly in the pregnancies of mothers over the age of 40.

Amniocentesis can detect not only Down's syndrome but also other chromosomal abnormalities that cause mental retardation, including trisomy 13, trisomy 18, *cri du chat* syndrome, and translocation Down's syndrome. It can also detect metabolic disorders that cause mental retardation, such as maple syrup urine disease and galactosemia.

There is a 1.5% chance of amniocentesis causing miscarriage after it is done, but for many people it may put to rest long-standing fears about their pregnancies. For some people, however, amniocentesis may confirm their worst fears. It is under these circumstances that mental retardation arouses its greatest controversy. Some couples, after hearing a diagnosis of mental retardation, choose to abort their fetus. While aborting a fetus is certainly never an easy decision to make, the fact that amniocentesis is done in the second trimester of pregnancy, when the mother is likely to be showing the pregnancy and the couple has had time to prepare themselves emotionally for the child, makes it even more difficult.

The second test mentioned above, chorionic villi sampling, has an advantage over amniocentesis in that it is done in the first trimester, from the 8th to 10th week of pregnancy. During CVS, a thin, tubelike structure is inserted vaginally into the mother. A small sample of chorionic villi (the cells that form the placenta) is then removed through the tube.

women, newborn infants, or older children. According to the Association for Retarded Citizens, germs, poor nutrition, injury, the ingestion of poisonous substances, and child abuse can all leave both the unborn and older child with a mental handicap. Perhaps the most tragic aspect of such instances is that many are avoidable.

According to statistics compiled by federal health officials, for example, it was estimated that 400,000 babies born in 1992 would develop chronic problems as the result of inadequate care before birth. Included on the list of infectious diseases that can result in a retarded infant if they strike a woman early in her pregnancy and damage her fetus are mumps, scarlet fever, whooping cough, measles, *rubella* (German measles), and meningitis.

The infectious disease known as *toxoplasmosis* can be acquired if a woman eats undercooked meat or comes into contact with soiled cat litter either before or during pregnancy. In such instances, the parasite that causes the disease can enter the woman's bloodstream and be passed on to her fetus. In the woman who contracts it, toxoplasmosis probably causes no more than a few days of flulike symptoms. The fetus of such a woman, however, can suffer from hydrocephalus or microcephaly (a smaller than normal head), as well as nerve damage.

Rubella is another acquired disease that can cause serious problems in the fetus of a woman who contracts the illness. If the disease is contracted in the first two months of pregnancy, the fetus has almost a 50% chance of having a rubella-related abnormality. The abnormalities caused by the disease can range from loss of hearing, heart problems, and cleft lips and palate to retardation. When a woman contracts rubella after the fourth month of pregnancy, the risk of such abnormalities developing in her fetus decreases dramatically.

Like toxoplasmosis, *cytomegalovirus* infection rarely produces symptoms in a pregnant woman. Yet it too, however, can cause severe retardation of the fetus if it is passed along.

Syphilis is a highly contagious, sexually transmitted disease that can affect the fetus of an infected woman. After the 18th week of gestation, at which time the *placenta* ceases to offer as much protection as it did in previous weeks, the fetus may readily contract the disease and experience severe retardation.

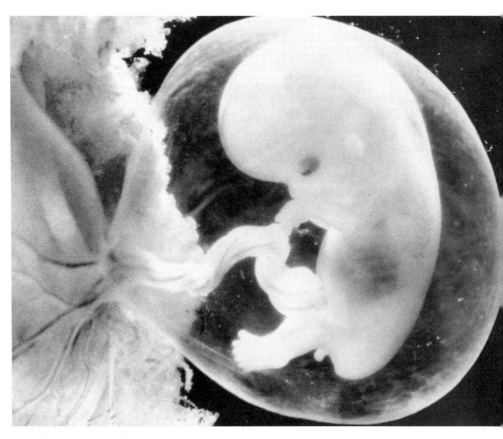

The developing embryo depends upon a complex and delicate group of special structures that sustain it and help to protect it against injury while it is in the uterus. As it floats inside the uterus, the fetus in this figure is surrounded by the fluid-filled amniotic sac. The umbilicus, which projects from the abdomen of the fetus, on the right, and passes down to the placenta at the bottom of the picture, contains blood vessels that carry nutrients into the fetus and transport wastes out of its body.

Both illicit and prescribed drugs, as well as environmental pollutants, can do serious harm to a developing fetus. This is because the fetus is, from the very beginning to the very last minute of a pregnancy, in a constant state of growth and development with its cells multiplying rapidly to create the organs, limbs, and systems needed to sustain the newly developing individual throughout life. Consequently, there is no safe or good time to use drugs, drink excessively, or be exposed to dangerous environmental factors during pregnancy. To understand why this is so, it is necessary to explain just how a fetus develops.

After an egg cell is fertilized in the mother's body, it develops the beginnings of the placenta, by which it attaches itself to the wall of the mother's uterus. The uterus, a pear-shaped organ, then carries the fetus until it is born approximately 40 weeks after fertilization.

The early embryo that will eventually develop into an infant is attached to the placenta by the umbilical cord, which extends from the placenta to the navel of the fetus. Although the mother's blood circulates through the placenta, providing nourishment for the fetus, and the fetus's blood also circulates through the placenta, picking up food from and eliminating wastes into the mother's blood, the two bloods almost never mix. Instead, the substances to be exchanged between the mother and fetus pass from one to the other by way of the placental tissues.

The placenta weighs up to one-fifth of what the fetus weighs and is vital to the fetus's survival. Should the placenta become infected or separate from the fetus, the fetus can die. Although the placenta stops growing at about the 34th week of gestation, it continues to provide nourishment for the fetus until birth. After the fetus is born, the placenta, sometimes called the afterbirth at this stage, passes out through the mother's birth canal.

Other specialized structures also help to keep the fetus safe. One of these is the amniotic sac, a thin membrane that surrounds the fetus and holds the amniotic fluid in which the fetus floats while in the womb.

Such shelter prevents most falls and even more serious injuries from affecting the fetus. It does not, however, prevent drugs and other toxic substances taken by the mother from passing into her bloodstream and traveling through her body and through the placenta into the fetus—a process that doctors often refer to as "crossing the placenta."

While many drugs pass through the placenta, the U.S. Food and Drug Administration has found that some, like penicillins and certain other antibiotics, cause no harm or birth defects in an unborn child. Still, most doctors prefer women to avoid using drugs during the crucial

WARNING!

COULD YOU BE PREGNANT?

DRINKING ALCOHOL CAN CAUSE BIRTH DEFECTS

FETAL ALCOHOL INFORMATION HOTLINE

1-800-532-6302

A poster warning women of childbearing age against the danger of birth defects caused by alcoholic beverages. Among the hazards of drinking during pregnancy are fetal alcohol syndrome, whose effects in newborn infants typically include a low birth weight, defects in hearing and sight, and mental retardation, among other abnormalities.

first trimester of pregnancy—the most rapid period of fetal growth. Some drugs, such as insulin for the treatment of diabetes, and certain medications used to treat epilepsy, must continue to be taken even during pregnancy, but in such cases the physician closely monitors the developing fetus's progress.

One of the environmental sources of mental retardation is nuclear radiation. The atomic bombs dropped on Hiroshima and Nagasaki, Japan, in August, 1945, caused severe retardation and other damage to many of the infants born to women who were pregnant at the time, some of whom are shown in this photograph.

Marijuana, cocaine, amphetamines, and other illicit drugs should be strictly avoided during pregnancy, since their use has been associated with low birth weights, withdrawal symptoms, lethargy, respiratory distress, chromosomal breakdown, and death in newborns. Even drugs that are harmless under other circumstances, such as

aspirin, may cause hemorrhaging in the fetus's brain if taken during pregnancy.

One widely used substance that has recently come to light as a potential source of serious birth defects, including retardation, is alcohol. According to the *Seventh Special Report to the U.S. Congress on Alcohol and Health, fetal alcohol syndrome*, or FAS, was first noted in the United States in 1973, when scientists observed a pattern in birth defects and other abnormalities among children born to mothers who drank heavily. The abnormalities included a low birth weight, developmental disabilities and delays, poor coordination, kidney problems, auditory impairment, visual problems, and facial deformity. When only some of these abnormalities are present, an infant is said to be suffering from *fetal alcohol effects*, or FAE, rather than FAS.

The report went on to designate FAS and FAE as leading causes of mental retardation in the Western world, which cost as much as three-quarters of $1 billion each year for the treatment of the children affected by them. The rates of FAS are higher in North America than in Europe or in other areas of the world: an estimated 1.9 out of every 1,000 live-born infants are affected with the disease. Among women who have four or more drinks of wine, hard liquor, or beer a day, the rate of FAS is believed to be as high as 25 per 1,000 births.

However, although an estimated 2.5% of all babies born to heavy-drinking mothers are born with FAS, scientists point out that others who escape the syndrome despite their mothers' heavy drinking may do so because certain genetic or physical differences in these mothers prevent their fetuses from being severely affected.

Metal poisoning is also capable of causing mental retardation. Lead poisoning, which mainly affects children living in inner-city slums who eat chips of lead-based paint, can cause irreparable brain damage and loss of intellectual capacity, even if only a small amount of such paint is ingested on each of several occasions. In addition, lead poisoning can cause anemia, miscarriage, hearing loss, depression, anxiety, seizures, coma, and even death. If discovered at an early stage, however, through the testing of the blood of children or adults, lead poisoning can be treated and the retardation it causes can be prevented with medication.

Other toxic substances that can impair intellectual functioning include mothballs, mercury, and nuclear wastes. In Hiroshima and Nagasaki, Japan, a large percentage of women who were pregnant when atomic bombs were dropped on these cities in August 1945, later gave birth to babies with abnormally small heads and with severe retardation.

The womb also cannot prevent the fetus from becoming malnourished. When a woman is pregnant, she is literally eating for two people. This does not mean that she must consume twice as much as usual, but rather that she must be extra careful to eat a good supply of nutritious foods each day. If she does not see to her nutritional needs, and starves herself to hide her pregnant figure or heedlessly feeds on calorie-laden but nutritionally poor foods, she will not only starve herself, but her unborn child as well.

Automobile and bicycle accidents, falls, and other mishaps that involve the head are also sources of brain injury and loss of intellectual functioning. According to the Ulster Association for Retarded Citizens, one child in every four suffers a preventable injury serious enough to

Sometimes simple friendship and caring are enough to make a difference in the life of a person who is intellectually disadvantaged.

require medical attention. Nearly 3,000 children in the United States require medical treatment each day for accidental injuries, with nearly 300 becoming permanently disabled.

According to the Ulster Association, another 6,000 children each year become disabled after being abused. Intentional severe blows to the head can easily cause brain damage, especially in a young child. Shaking an infant is now known to cause a swelling of brain tissue, resulting in brain damage and in some cases death. In recent years, this sad phenomenon has happened so frequently that it has been named the *shaken baby syndrome*.

Once mental retardation is definitely established it is necessary to plan appropriate care for the affected individual. In most cases, this includes education and training. Chapter 4 will discuss the education of retarded children.

EDUCATION AND TESTING IN MENTAL RETARDATION

A special education teacher working on a word-puzzle game with an elderly man who has mental disabilities. When special education for people with mental disabilities was begun in the early 20th century, its teachers had to be drawn from the ranks of kindergarten and primary-grade school teachers.

The turn of the 20th century saw the first public-school programs for retarded children in the United States. By 1922, 23 states had public-education programs for the mentally retarded.

In 1911, New Jersey passed the first state law requiring special education for the retarded, and 13 states followed with similar laws by

1922. By the mid-1920s, it had become evident that the state rather than the federal government was going to be responsible for the education of the retarded. But although the special education bandwagon continued to grow, the newly developing programs contained problems that were to be ignored for years.

The purpose of the first special education classes was largely to remove unwanted students from regular classes rather than to educate the retarded. These unwanted students included children who were violent or disruptive, and who in turn became a problem in special education.

Problems persisted even when special education began to increase its focus on retarded children, rather than those in need of control. Children with physical problems both severe and mild were lumped together, along with those who were mentally handicapped.

Another problem was that some schools made their choices for special education strictly on the basis of a child's intelligence quotient, or IQ, in which the level of intellectual function was determined to be appropriate, advanced, or retarded for the child's age. Rather than taking those children with IQs on the higher end of the scale, these schools instead took children at the lower end of the scale, and used school as a bridge to institutionalization. The school days for children who were deemed retarded were also hours shorter than ordinary classes and were divided evenly among schoolwork, grooming tips, and the domestic arts.

Nor could the parents of retarded children agree on what they wanted. Some wanted special classes in the community's regular schools, so that their children could learn to socialize. Others wanted segregated schools so that their children would only be with other retarded children.

Furthermore, when special education was created, there were no special educators. Most of the earliest teachers in such programs were taken from the ranks of kindergarten or primary grade teachers. In 1902, the Vineland Training School in New Jersey offered the first training course for special education teachers. By 1909, recognizing that courses in psychology as well as in regular teaching methods were needed to teach the retarded, most large cities began requiring special examinations and licenses for special education teachers. By 1930, 10 states required special education teachers to have certification. By 1934, over 80,000 students were enrolled in special education programs throughout the United States.

The 1950s saw changes in the goals of special education. No longer were classes for the retarded to be used as a means of segregating them within institutions. Rather, it began to be established that such classes were to be used to prepare mildly retarded children to eventually reenter the community and live and work among their normal peers. Those with more severe retardation, or the trainable retarded, were to be taught as best they could the things they would need to function on a daily basis, even though it was recognized that they would not be self-supporting. By 1963, 361,000 students were being educated in special classes.

In 1975, with passage of the Education for All Handicapped Children Act, a free and appropriate education was guaranteed for all children regardless of any handicap they might have. In 1986, the 1975 act was expanded to include children who were not yet identified as having a disability but who were considered at risk for one. It is now known that *early intervention*, the prompt diagnosis and treatment of retardation, can greatly increase a child's chance of developing more normally. With such intervention the child's parents and educators cooperate in providing him or her with appropriate physical and mental exercises, such as stimulating visual displays for an infant and challenging physical exercises for a toddler.

Early intervention is based on the principle that with intensive help, retarded children can come closer to meeting the milestones of childhood development at the same time as their normal peers. They are taught muscle coordination, fine motor control, and the alphabet, just like other children, but at an earlier age and in a series of repetitious exercises that helps them to better remember what they are taught. As a result, more retarded children today are reaching their full potential.

The parental involvement that begins with the early intervention program does not end once the child is ready for grade school. The

Education for All Handicapped Children Act guarantees that all children must be fairly tested, with tests that show their strengths as well as their weaknesses, before they are recommended for a certain program. And parents have the right to challenge those recommendations by taking their case before a mediator.

TESTING FOR RETARDATION

As we discussed earlier, the parents of a retarded child may note certain delays in the child's development that alert them to a problem. In some

A class where intellectually handicapped children are integrated into a normal learning environment. The Education for All Handicapped Children Act, passed in 1975, guarantees a free and appropriate education for all children, including those with mental retardation.

cases, though, the delay is mild, and often is not noted until the child is of school age. Regardless of when a delay is first suspected, appropriate testing is available. Testing is a necessary part of the special education process, for without it, the child cannot receive the right kind of help.

The three most common tests used for determining a child's abilities are the *Bayley Scales*, the *Stanford-Binet Scale*, and the *Wechsler Scales*.

The Bayley Scales are used for children of two months to two-and-a-half years of age and involve different levels of play. Because these

An infant with metnal disabilities is shown pictures by a special education counselor. The concept of early intervention involves the use of stimulating visual displays, challenging physical exercises, and other appropriate means of fostering the intellectual growth of infants and toddlers who are mentally disabled.

scales do not test for language development, the results often vary from those of later tests. Severe retardation, however, is usually not hard to predict.

The Stanford-Binet Scale picks up where the Bayley Scales leave off, at two-and-a-half years old. The Stanford-Binet Scale primarily tests a child's verbal development and reasoning ability.

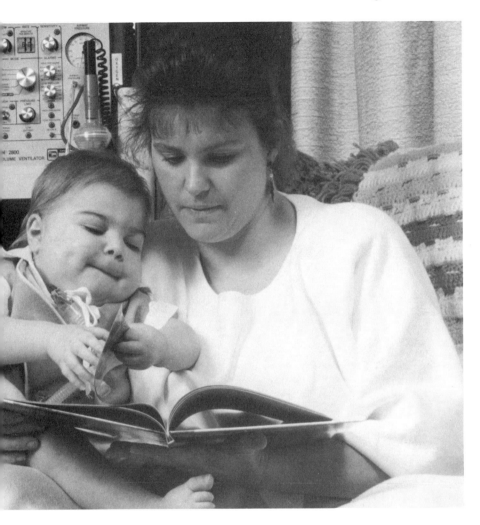

The Wechsler Scales are the ones most commonly used after a child has reached school age. Created by American psychologist David Wechsler, they include two parts, one that tests verbal ability and one that measures performance.

The Wechsler Pre-School and Primary Scale of Intelligence is used for children up to age 6, while the Revised Wechsler Intelligence Scale for Children is used for youngsters up to age 16. The Wechsler Adult Intelligence Scale is used for persons 16 and older. A child who has been tested and is determined to be retarded is eligible for certain programs. Early intervention for an infant or toddler may take place in the home or at a special center, one or two days a week. In addition, parents are taught a series of exercises that they can do with their

A retarded youngster working at a computer. Training schools for retarded children offer instruction and experience in specialized skills that can later be used in a sheltered job setting or in the nation's general work force.

children at home to help them develop more rapidly than they otherwise might before they start school.

An older retarded child who is already enrolled in school can also be entered into a special program, which can range from special education classes to a combination of special classes and regular classes to a full schedule of regular classes. The programs for which a retarded child is eligible are determined by the results of various tests. In addition to the tests described above, a child's social history and psychological well-being are examined by an assigned team. This evaluation often includes having a sociologist visit the child's family and make a report. The report will probably include testing by the school psychologist. As a result of the evaluation, the child may be given such additional help as vocational training, speech therapy, or physical therapy.

If the parents do not agree with the results of the tests, or do not wish the school to test their child, they have the option of taking their child to an independent testing facility.

The *individualized education program*, or IEP, that is recommended for a particular child is created by both the child's parents and professional personnel, and includes educational goals and such further services as vocational training.

The IEP also indicates the amount of time a retarded student will be in classes with normal students. Known as *mainstreaming*, this is a right guaranteed by the Education for All Handicapped Children Act. While in the past, school systems may have wished to segregate retarded children by sending them to specialized schools, these children now have the right to attend regular classes in the same schools as other children their age.

Even if a child has been enrolled in a special education program, he or she is not stuck there indefinitely. Under the federal handicapped education act, a school must review a student's IEP annually, checking progress and determining whether the choices made are still valid. If not, new courses of action can be taken. Teachers can also ask that a student be retested for admission to a normal school program.

With enough educational resources, youngsters with intellectual handicaps can make achievements beyond all expectation.

According to special education authorities Winifred Anderson, Stephen Chitwood, and Deidre Hayden, the IEP should include six parts. The first part is a description of the child and should include his or her level of education, behavior, strengths, and weaknesses.

The second part of the IEP is a list of goals or objectives. Such goals, say Anderson, Chitwood, and Hayden, should be short-term and highly specific. "Janie will play well with two girls her own age for short periods, by May" is an example of a specific and constructive goal, as opposed to the vague "Janie will increase her ability to interact with others."

The third part of the IEP involves the grade level at which the child will be placed. This is determined by the child's strengths and needs. Today, more retarded children are taking some or all of their classes with their normal peers so that they are better prepared to enter society and live and work independently.

Special-education classes can teach intellectually handicapped children how to cope with everyday experiences, such as talking on the telephone.

The fourth part of the IEP is a listing of additional services to be rendered to the child, which can include counseling, transportation, or specific therapies. The fifth part of the IEP specifies the duration of a particular component of the treatment program. For example, it might be noted that the child will attend special classes for the next school year. These goals are projected only a year or so in advance, since the entire IEP must be evaluated annually, and the child's needs may change.

The sixth and last part of the IEP is the evaluation of the program's effectiveness for the child. This is done each year to see whether the child's needs are being met. Either the parent or the school may request such a review, however, at any time they feel it is necessary.

In addition to special education, training schools exist for more severely retarded children. These programs offer practical training in skills that can some day be used in a sheltered job setting, or even in the regular work force, for students who may have difficulty in ever learning to read or even to speak properly.

Adult education is also within the reach of the mentally retarded. Vocational schools offer post–high school training in health and hygiene, and cosmetic, business, and secretarial skills. Moreover, a number of colleges and universities now offer programs designed for mentally handicapped students.

CHAPTER 5

LIVING ARRANGEMENTS

A young winner in an athletic meet for persons with intellectual disabilities. Many parents who might have once sent these children to institutions now take them home to lead lives more nearly like those of ordinary youngsters.

Before public education became the lawful right of retarded children, only a few private schools in the country could serve this special population, and these were extremely limited in size and resources. Almost nothing was known about educating a retarded child in the home, much less about early intervention.

Today, there is little reason why a person suffering from retardation can not be trained to be self-supporting.

The change began when parents started to hear negative reports about the institutions that were once the only treatment facilities for the retarded. The media began producing these reports in the 1970s describing how institutionalized retarded children were being drugged, beaten, and left unwashed. The reports also noted that many of the institutions' residents died young, often by the age of 20, and most by middle age.

As these stories alerted parents to the horrors of the institutions that held their children, more of them began keeping their retarded children at home. With the help of persons who dedicated their lives to helping retarded children, these parents discovered that retarded people, although different, did not have to be feared or scorned. The majority

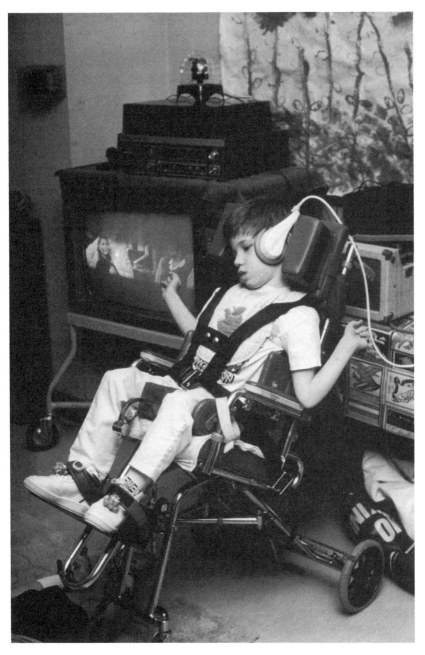

Modern technology can give a child suffering from retardation more control over his or her world than was ever before possible.

GENETICS

The following exercise can help you to better understand genetics and the principle of dominant and recessive genes.

Imagine that your mother and father both have brown eyes. Sometime before you were born, they probably wondered what color eyes you would have.

Many people, knowing that your parents both have brown eyes, would probably answer that you, too, would share your parents' brown eye color. That assumption, however, would not be entirely correct.

To understand this, we must first take a look at your grandparents' eye color. For the sake of argument, let us say that both of your grandfathers have brown eyes, but that each of them also carries a gene for blue eyes. Let us also assume that both of your grandmothers have blue eyes.

This would mean that while both of your parents are brown-eyed, each of them also carries a blue-eye gene and a brown-eye gene.

The blue-eye genes, while they may not have affected your parents, can certainly affect you. To calculate the probability that you will have blue eyes, you will have to create a small chart called a checkerboard, or a Punnett square, like the one shown below.

On the left side of the chart are the eye-color genes your mother has inherited. As you can see, the large *B* represents brown eye color, governed by a gene that she inherited from her father, and the small *b* represents blue eye color, which she inherited from her mother.

The top of the chart represents your father's eye-color genes. Here again you will see a large *B* for the brown-eye-color gene that your father inherited from your brown-eyed grandfather, and a small *b* representing the blue-eye gene he inherited from your grandmother.

The four squares of the chart contain the possible combinations that can result from the union of your mother and father's eye-color genes. The top left square represents the possibility of a brown-eyed child—one who has two dominant brown-eye genes and does not carry the recessive blue-eye gene. The lower left square also represents the possibility of a brown-eyed child. This time, however, the child carries one dominant brown-eye gene and one recessive blue-eye gene. The upper right corner of the square represents the same possibility as the lower left—a brown-eyed child who also carries the recessive blue-eye gene. The lower right square, however, represents a blue-eyed child, the product of the coming together of your parents' recessive blue-eye genes. In fact, the only way a child can have blue eyes, as you may have guessed, is to carry two recessive blue-eye genes.

You may have also already guessed that there was a 75% chance of your being a brown-eyed child and only a 25% chance of your having blue eyes. This does not mean, however, that if your parents were to have four children, three of them would be brown-eyed and one would be blue-eyed. All it means is that each child your parents have has a 75% chance of having brown eyes and only a 25% chance of having blue eyes.

Father's Eye Color		
	B	b
B	BB	Bb
b	Bb	bb

Mother's Eye Color

B = brown eyes (dominant)
b = blue eyes (recessive)

were not violent, any more than are most humans. They did not want to hurt anyone, but instead to give love to and care for others.

Today, in most cases retarded people are no longer considered an embarrassment to their families or to society. Most families of retarded infants now bring them home, where they are raised with their siblings. They attend early intervention programs, and later go to school. Many then go on to hold jobs, marry and have children, and engage in a wide range of social activities and personal interests.

Much of this progress is due to the more varied living options now available to the retarded. Many retarded people, with their families, are able to choose from a wide selection the residential situation best suited to their needs.

A group home within the general community is one of the modern options available to persons with mental disabilities who require regular medical or personal supervision. In this picture, the group supervisor is teaching a resident of a group home to play checkers.

Persons with mental disabilities working in a manufacturing plant sewing surgical garments. Today, many individuals with mental disabilities hold jobs in the private sector, and a number of companies offer special vocational programs for them.

The most advanced of all living options for a retarded individual is that of living independently. This is a viable option for those with very mild retardation. For most others, however, some degree of supervision is required. Some housing plans allow retarded persons to live in an apartment, usually with one or two roommates. There they can do their own shopping, cooking, and cleaning, but they also receive periodic visits from an appointed supervisor.

For those who wish to live in a community but need additional attention, either personal or medical, a group home is a good option. These homes often house from six to a dozen residents. They can help with the housework and the cooking, but they have round-the-clock house parents. Many retarded residents of both apartments and group homes work in the communities in which they live. Some are paid employees in sheltered workshops, where, for instance, they may help assemble shaving kits or put together doorbells.

Other retarded individuals hold down jobs in the private sector, working at fast food restaurants, answering telephones in an office, or doing more advanced work if their abilities allow. Many companies

offer special programs for disabled persons. One such program is McJobs, offered by the McDonald's corporation. A community's local ARC chapter can provide detailed information about such programs in its region.

In addition to the housing and employment options available to retarded persons, local organizations offer daytime treatment programs, weekend events, and even social gatherings. Such organiza-

Group settings can help people with intellectual disabilities to function better and to learn the skills of forming social relationships.

tions can be located through state or community mental health departments or the national ARC office.

For severely retarded persons who are multiply handicapped or suffering from some form of mental illness, residence in an institution offering skilled nursing care and supervision may be the most suitable option. Such institutions, although still far from perfect, are today required to follow strict regulations with regard to the quality of care they provide, and they are periodically examined to ensure that this is the case. Many institutions have made an effort to appear brighter and more homelike than they once did, and most offer a wide range of planned activities. Visits by the residents' families and the families' participation in the residents' care are still recommended. It is important that the family keep an eye on the quality of care the retarded individual is receiving. Signs of abuse or neglect should be immediately reported to social workers or the institution's directors.

CHAPTER 6

INTO THE LIGHT

Two men with mental retardation watching a baseball game. Today, mental retardation need not affect an individual's ability to enjoy life and be a productive member of a community.

In the past, mental retardation was a harsh sentence that heralded a future with little or no personal accomplishment. In most cases, retarded children were put into an institution, destined to spend the remainder of their days under sedation intended to prevent them from causing trouble, and staring blankly into space.

Today, mental retardation need not interfere with the affected individual's ability to enjoy life and to be a productive member of a community. The mentally handicapped can now obtain education, and some even go to college. Many hold down jobs and live in homes in their communities. Some marry, and a few have children. And there are scientists who believe that the situation for the retarded can get even better.

VITAMIN THERAPY

In 1981, a group of researchers led by Professor Ruth F. Harrell at Old Dominion University in Norfolk, Virginia, reported that they had found

A poster warns against child abuse. Physical abuse at a young age can contribute to retardation and intellectual dysfunction.

When you're angry, don't shake your baby . . . reach for help.

Phone the child abuse TALK line in your area.

April is Child Abuse Prevention Month

Prepared as a public service by the California Medical Association

a way to improve the intellectual capacity of retarded children through vitamin and mineral supplements.

Although scientists had long theorized that a lack of some nutrients could cause retardation, there had been no proof that this was actually the case. However, over an eight-month period, Harrell and her colleagues gave one group of mentally retarded children, including some with Down's syndrome, huge daily doses of vitamins A, B, C, D, and E, as well as minerals such as iron, calcium, and zinc.

The results were astonishing. The children's IQs rose considerably, increasing in at least one case of a child with Down's syndrome by 25 points. Many of the treated children were able to enter regular classes.

There were also physical benefits from the treatment. Two children with Down's syndrome lost the characteristic bloated look that accompanies the disease. Others reported improved eyesight. Further evidence supporting the treatment regimen came when some children reportedly fell back to their former level of functioning when the program ended.

Although these findings appear promising, however, they must be corroborated. So far, the few tests that have followed Harrell's have failed to show the same extraordinary results.

PREVENTION

According to the Association for Retarded Citizens, prevention is possible in nearly half of the cases of retardation that occur each year as a result of accidents and environmental factors, such as lead poisoning and fetal alcohol syndrome.

Lead poisoning can be prevented by inspecting buildings to see if they have been painted with paint that contains lead. If they do, all flaking paint should be scraped off and the affected surfaces repainted with a latex paint. For a child who may have consumed lead, a local poison control hotline can provide immediate assistance, and the local department of health can offer more information.

Retardation caused by PKU, galactosemia, hypothyroidism, and other metabolic diseases can be prevented simply by making sure that each newborn is tested for these abnormalities. Such screening is mandatory in most of the United States, as well as in Canada and parts of Europe, and is done unless the parents object to it for religious reasons. The tests are generally performed on the third day of the baby's life and involve only the pricking of the baby's heel so that a blood sample can be taken. The sample is put on a small piece of filter paper, which is then sent to a regional laboratory for analysis. If the baby tests positively for any of the above-mentioned conditions, treatment can begin immediately before any damage is done. In communities in which newborn screening is not a routine procedure, a pediatrician can provide the names of physicians or facilities in which it can be done.

Child abuse and neglect are also, obviously, preventable sources of retardation. Either can cause injury to a child's head. Infants have little muscle development in or control over their heads, and as a result are extremely prone to injuries to the head and neck. Shaking can damage the soft tissue of the brain and bruising can cause swelling. If the brain swells greatly, it can become compressed against the bones of the skull, causing brain damage.

Child abuse is a criminal offense, and few parents or caretakers will admit to it. Unfortunately, this might prevent them from seeking attention for a child who has been seriously injured. Counseling for parents and others who abuse children is now available in virtually every area of the United States. Anyone in need of counseling, or who believes that a child they know is being abused, should contact a child abuse hotline or the police. For advice about counseling, they should contact their local mental health association.

Infants and toddlers, as they begin to wander about on unsteady legs, are accident prone, as well. A child who falls and hits his or her head may suffer a serious injury. A fall from a bicycle at 20 miles per hour, which is the speed at which most children ride their bikes, can be fatal. Protective headgear greatly reduces the risk of head injury during bicycling. If a child suffers a fall of any kind and afterward seems drowsy and lethargic, is difficult to awaken, vomits, has dilated pupils, or exhibits disorientation or other unusual behavior, medical attention should be gotten immediately.

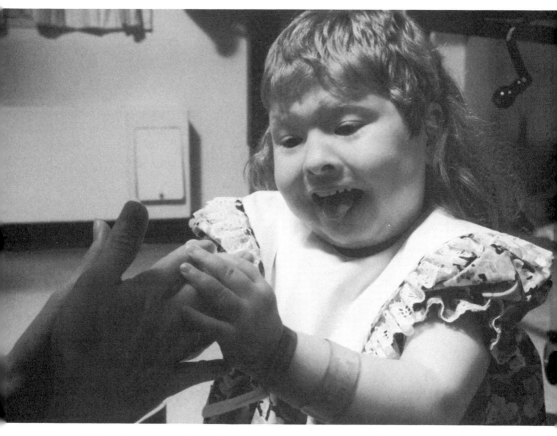

A child with mental disabilities learning to count on a therapist's fingers. Genetic counseling can prepare prospective parents for the birth of an infant with mental disabilities and help them to plan in advance for his or her education and upbringing.

Both accidents and abuse can occur when a child is still in the womb. Some mothers may take prescription drugs or over-the-counter remedies before realizing that they are pregnant. Others drink or abuse drugs despite the knowledge that they are pregnant.

Recently, judges in some states have set a legal precedent by jailing mothers who have taken illicit drugs while knowing they are pregnant.

The judges' argument is that these mothers are guilty of child abuse. In general, it is also recommended that a pregnant woman refrain from drinking, since it is not yet known whether even moderate drinking can harm a developing fetus.

According to the results of the 1985 National Health Survey, 84% of the 20,000 men and women aged 18 to 44 who were questioned were aware that heavy drinking can cause problems during pregnancy. However, only 55% of those surveyed had heard of fetal alcohol syndrome, and only one-fourth of the survey respondents knew that birth defects are a symptom of the disease.

The only way to avoid such endangerment of the fetus is through better prenatal care and education. To make the public more aware of the dangers of drinking during pregnancy, in 1989 the federal government began requiring all manufacturers of alcoholic beverages to display warnings on the beverage containers pointing out the risks of drinking while pregnant. Education in schools is also needed to ensure that young people understand the dangers of drinking to a developing fetus. The library is another good source of information, as is a prenatal clinic. An obstetrician can advise a mother-to-be about such matters as alcohol consumption, nutrition, and desired weight gain during pregnancy.

The recommendations for alcohol apply to all drugs, as well. Because they cross the placenta, drugs can have the same effects on a fetus as they do on the mother. And with the fetus weighing only a fraction of the mother's weight, these effects can be greatly magnified, dramatically damaging organs and systems that are developing rapidly.

With recent cutbacks in federal, state, and local government spending, however, prenatal care for mothers at high risk for fetal retardation is itself at risk. Most public clinics are federally funded, and are already overworked and understaffed. Cutbacks threaten the level of care for both parents and their unborn children.

GENETIC COUNSELING

In order to limit instances of retardation with a genetic basis, prenatal testing has come into wide use. For prospective parents who are concerned about having a child with a disability, awareness can begin even before pregnancy, with *genetic counseling*. Genetic counseling is recommended for all parents who have already had a child with a disability, who believe that they may be carriers of a hereditary disease, or who have had relatives with various diseases, as well as those who are older and concerned about the risks of having a child when the woman is over the age of 35.

Mentally retarded children being taught to paint in an art class. From infancy to old age, retarded persons are today living fuller lives than they ever have before.

In genetic counseling, both prospective parents provide complete personal health histories, including that of relatives on both sides of the family. A physical examination is also done on each parent to determine whether he or she has any unrecognized health problems. A variety of tests may also be performed.

Genetic counseling can inform parents about their chances of conceiving a handicapped child and about the kinds of diseases or handicaps he or she might have. This enables the couple to make an informed decision about whether or not to have a child.

Genetic counseling can also put a couple's fears to rest. A parent may remember an aunt who was always slow, or a cousin with a particular disease. With genetic counseling, the couple may discover that neither of them carries the genetic blueprints for any such problem or disease, and can safely conceive a child. Couples who have one handicapped child may discover that its affliction is not a genetic one and that their next child is unlikely to be affected. A gynecologist or family physician can provide more detailed information to couples who wish to have genetic counseling.

LOOKING AHEAD

The future for retarded persons seems bright. New research on retardation is underway in the areas of genetics, psychology, and neurology, and scientists already know more about mental retardation than was once ever thought possible.

Retarded people are also leading fuller lives than they did only a short while ago, with careers, friends, and responsibilities. They have come far from the prisonlike institutions of only a few short decades ago.

APPENDIX

FOR MORE INFORMATION

The following is a list of organizations that can provide further information about mental retardation and related topics.

GENERAL INFORMATION

American Association on Mental Retardation
1719 Kalorama Road NW
Washington, DC 20009
(202) 387-1968

Council for Exceptional Children
1920 Association Drive
Reston, VA 22091-1589
(703) 620-3660

National Association for Retarded Citizens (ARC)
500 East Border Street, suite 300
Arlington, TX 76010
(800) 433-5255

President's Committee on Mental Retardation
330 Independence Avenue SW
The Wilber J. Cohen Building, room 5325
Washington, DC 20201
(202) 619-0634

Special Olympics, Inc.
1350 New York Avenue NW, suite 500
Washington, DC 20005
(202) 628-3630

CEREBRAL PALSY

American Academy for Cerebral Palsy and Developmental Medicine
P.O. Box 11086
Richmond, VA 23230-0186
(804) 282-0036

United Cerebral Palsy Association
120 East 23rd Street
New York, NY 10010
(212) 979-9700

DOWN'S SYNDROME

National Down's Syndrome Congress
1800 Depster Street
Park Ridge, IL 60068
(800) 232-NDSC (6372)

National Down's Syndrome Society
666 Broadway, suite 810
New York, NY 10012
(212) 460-9330

FETAL ALCOHOL SYNDROME AND DRUG USE

National Clearinghouse for Alcohol and
  Drug Information
11426 Rockville Pike
Rockville, MD 20852
(301) 468-2600

FURTHER READING

Anderson, Winifred, Stephen Chitwood, and Deidre Hayden. *Negotiating the Special Education Maze*. Kensington, MD: Woodbine House, 1990.

Batshaw, Mark L., M.D. *Your Child Has A Disability*. Boston: Little, Brown, 1991.

Berger, Melvin. *Hazardous Substances*. Hillside, NJ: Enslow, 1986.

Busselle, Rebecca. *An Exposure of the Heart*. New York: Norton, 1989.

Cipriano, Robert E. *Special Olympics*. Guilford, CT: Special Learning Corporation, 1980.

Cunningham, Cliff. *Down's Syndrome*. Cambridge, MA: Brookline Books, 1987.

Cunningham, Cliff, and Patricia Sloper. *Helping Your Exceptional Baby*. New York: Pantheon Books, 1980.

Egg, Maria. *When a Child is Different*. New York: John Day, 1964.

Jordan, Thomas Edward. *The Mentally Retarded*. Columbus, OH: Merrill, 1976.

Mercer, Jane R. *Labeling the Mentally Retarded*. Berkeley: University of California Press, 1973.

O'Reilly, Diane. *Retard*. Macomb, IL: Glenbridge, 1989.

Ross, Bette M. *Our Special Child*. New York: Walker, 1981.

Scheerenberger, R.C. *A History of Mental Retardation*. Baltimore: P. H. Brookes, 1983.

Zigler, Edward, and Robert M. Hodapp. *Understanding Mental Retardation*. New York: Cambridge University Press, 1986.

GLOSSARY

amniocentesis a test for genetic defects in an unborn child; chromosomes in fetal cells drawn from fluid inside the birth sac are examined for abnormalities; it cannot be performed until the mother is 14 to 16 weeks into a pregnancy

Bayley Scales a test for mental retardation in children aged two months to two-and-a-half years

cerebral palsy a nervous system disorder resulting from damage that occurs before or during birth; it leaves the child partially paralyzed, with poor muscle coordination, and, in some cases, mentally retarded

chorionic villi sampling (CVS) a method of testing for genetic defects very early in a pregnancy (8 to 10 weeks); the villi (tiny fingerlike projections found in the placenta) are removed and their chromosomes are examined

chromosome the rodlike structures of DNA and protein found in the nucleus of mammalian cells; each normal human cell contains 23 pairs of chromosomes (except gametes, which hold 23 single chromosomes)

congenital existing prior to or at birth

cretinism a term used to describe the combination of physical and mental defects caused by hypothyroidism

cri du chat syndrome a birth defect that results from having an incomplete number 5 chromosome

cytomegalovirus any of several herpes viruses that cause severe disease and brain damage in newborns

deinstitutionalization the policy of allowing mentally retarded people to live at home or in the community rather than in an institution

deletion abnormality a genetic abnormality that occurs when a person has only a fraction of a complete chromosome; the more complete the chromosomal fragment, the less severe the abnormality

Down's syndrome a variety of congenital mental retardation that ranges from moderate to severe; it is caused by the presence of an extra chromosome 21 and is marked by certain physical abnormalities

early intervention special education classes or programs that begin immediately after birth, filling the gap between diagnosis of mental disability and school

fetal alcohol effects (FAE) a condition in which an infant suffers from some of the symptoms of FAS

fetal alcohol syndrome (FAS) a set of birth defects associated with heavy drinking by pregnant women; symptoms include low birth weight, developmental delays, auditory problems, and facial deformity

fragile X syndrome a common inherited cause of mental retardation; results from a weakness in an abnormal X chromosome that causes it to break

galactose a complex sugar that forms when the body breaks down lactose, a sugar found in milk

galactosemia a disease caused by the inability of the body to break down galactose; it can cause mental retardation, cataracts, and possibly death if left untreated, but it can be treated through a special diet

genetic inherited; concerning defects or abnormalities of chromosomal material

genetic counseling a counseling session in which prospective parents share their family medical records and undergo physical examinations and tests in order to determine if they are carrying genetic traits for handicaps that they could pass on to their unborn child

hereditary inherited

hydrocephalus the buildup of spinal fluid in the brain, which distorts the head and damages brain tissue; it is often caused in the fetus by toxoplasmosis

hypothyroidism a condition caused by an underactive thyroid gland, resulting in a low forehead, thick lips, a protruding tongue, stunted stature, and mental retardation

individualized education program (IEP) the educational plan that is drawn up as a result of testing a developmentally disabled child and discussion between his or her parents and members of a team appointed by the school board in the child's area; the plan includes reasonable goals for the child, a listing of the student's strengths and weaknesses, and any additional services the child is entitled to

Klinefelter's syndrome a condition suffered only by males born with an extra X chromosome; it causes sterility and mental retardation and may result in a feminine appearance

mainstreaming the placing of mentally retarded children into classes with normal children their age

maple syrup urine disease a rare, inherited disease that prohibits the body from breaking down four amino acids; if left untreated, it is fatal, but it can be treated with a special diet if diagnosed early enough

melancholia the ancient Greek term for depression

mental retardation a condition that is said to be present when one's IQ is lower than 70; it can be a result of a birth defect, trauma, injury, or a number of other factors; there are four recognized levels of retardation—mild, moderate, severe, and profound

metabolic concerning the bodily processes for handling substances, either to create useful substances or to excrete harmful ones

mongolism the original name for Down's syndrome; the term comes from the supposedly Mongoloid appearance of those affected with the disease

phenylalanine an amino acid that is harmless in normal humans but that builds up in the bloodstreams of individuals with PKU, damaging brain tissue and causing retardation

phenylketonuria (PKU) a disease resulting from the absence of an enzyme that allows the body to break down phenylalanine; if it is diagnosed early enough, PKU can be treated by eliminating phenylalanine from the diet

placenta the organ that develops during pregnancy to supply the fetus with oxygen, food, water, and nutrients from the mother's bloodstream and to carry waste back to the mother's body for disposal

prenatal testing the examination of fetal cells to screen for birth defects or to determine gender

radioimmunoassay a screening procedure for hypothyroidism, PKU, and other diseases; a small amount of an infant's blood is tested a few days after birth

Rh factor a chemical substance found in the red blood cells of some people

Rh incompatibility a condition in which the red blood cells from an Rh-positive fetus enter the bloodstream of an Rh-negative mother, triggering destructive antibodies that can endanger the fetus, as well as future pregnancies with Rh-positive fetuses

rubella German measles; an acute infectious disease that can cause birth defects, including mental retardation, if the mother contracts it during pregnancy

shaken baby syndrome the swelling of and damage to the brain and neck caused by the shaking of a small child

Stanford-Binet Scale a test for mental retardation in children from two-and-a-half years of age to school age

syphilis a bacterial, sexually transmitted disease, which if left untreated can be fatal; it can also cause death or serious birth defects in a fetus who contracts the disease through an infected mother

thyroid gland an endocrine gland located at the base of the neck; it regulates growth and many of the metabolic processes

toxoplasmosis an infectious disease that can cause severe brain damage to a fetus when contracted from the mother; common sources of toxoplasmosis for adults are cat litter and undercooked meat

translocation abnormality a genetic abnormality that occurs when a portion of one chromosome is somehow removed and transferred to another chromosome

translocation Down's syndrome a usually mild form of Down's syndrome caused by the translocation of part of the number 21 chromosome to either the number 14 or 15 chromosome

trephination an early type of brain surgery performed in South America in which the patient's skull was opened to release evil spirits believed to be causing mental problems

trisomy a genetic disorder where three chromosomes exist instead of the normal pair; some of the more common trisomies are trisomy 21 (Down's syndrome), trisomy 13 (Patau's syndrome), and trisomy 18

Turner's syndrome the absence of an X chromosome in females; it can result in short stature, sterility, and various learning disorders

Wechsler Scales two sets of tests that determine mental retardation; the first is for children up to age 6, and the second is for those up to age 16

X chromosome a sex chromosome in human beings that usually occurs paired in each female cell and single in each male cell

Y chromosome a sex chromosome in human beings that usually occurs only in the male and is paired with an X chromosome in each cell

zygote the earliest stages of the embryo

INDEX

PICTURE CREDITS

Laura Dolce is the author of *Suicide* in the Chelsea House ENCYCLOPEDIA OF HEALTH series, as well as *Australia* from the Chelsea House PLACES AND PEOPLES OF THE WORLD series. She received her B.A. in communications from Fordham University in 1986. She currently works as a free-lance writer and editor and lives in Middletown, New York, with her husband and daughter.

Dale C. Garell, M.D., is medical director of California Children Services, Department of Health Services, County of Los Angeles. He is also associate dean for curriculum at the University of Southern California School of Medicine and clinical professor in the Department of Pediatrics & Family Medicine at the University of Southern California School of Medicine. From 1963 to 1974, he was medical director of the Division of Adolescent Medicine at Children's Hospital in Los Angeles. Dr. Garell has served as president of the Society for Adolescent Medicine, chairman of the youth committee of the American Academy of Pediatrics, and as a forum member of the White House Conference on Children (1970) and White House Conference on Youth (1971). He has also been a member of the editorial board of the *American Journal of Diseases of Children.*

C. Everett Koop, M.D., Sc.D., is former Surgeon General, deputy assistant secretary for health, and director of the Office of International Health of the U.S. Public Health Service. A pediatric surgeon with an international reputation, he was previously surgeon-in-chief of Children's Hospital of Philadelphia and professor of pediatric surgery and pediatrics at the University of Pennsylvania. Dr. Koop is the author of more than 175 articles and books on the practice of medicine. He has served as surgery editor of the *Journal of Clinical Pediatrics* and editor-in-chief of the *Journal of Pediatric Surgery.* Dr. Koop has received nine honorary degrees and numerous other awards, including the Denis Brown Gold Medal of the British Association of Paediatric Surgeons, the William E. Ladd Gold Medal of the American Academy of Pediatrics, and the Copernicus Medal of the Surgical Society of Poland. He is a chevalier of the French Legion of Honor and a member of the Royal College of Surgeons, London.